For Jenny Ng,
my friend and the best co-pilot any author
could possibly wish for

Contents

CONTENTS

So Why Did You Write the Book, Fergus?

This book had a simple and – rather obvious – birth.

I was thinking one day about how I'd really like to be nineteen again. Nineteen – but to have all the knowledge about the world that I have gained – gained from people I've met or been involved with, gained from situations I've been in or experienced, gained from the countless dumb mistakes that I've made.

It occurred to me then that a book that talked about this knowledge – but in a business context – would be a useful thing. I've made lots of mistakes in my working life – some big, plenty small. If a book could stop other people from making those mistakes then that probably would be a good enough reason to destroy a lot of trees and make a book. You'll be able to make plenty mistakes of your own. You don't have to make the ones I made.

Mistakes involve waste – sometimes appalling amounts of it. And waste, of course, is one of the big problems in the world today. I don't just mean rubbish/garbage, but waste of time, effort, resources, money, people, lives. If a book like this could stop some of that waste then the destruction of the trees – not really a good thing – would have been repaid by these savings – which could be a very good thing indeed.

That was good enough for me. I pitched it to Darin, my agent. He liked it. We pitched it to the good folks at Wiley. *They* liked it. I got to work and here we are.

Thank you for buying and I hope it makes a difference.

Fergus O'Connell
Ireland, 2015

OK, So What's the Plan?

Maybe you've started working for somebody else – a company or organization. Maybe you've started your own thing. In either case I think you'll find much that will be of use to you in this book. (And given that I've done both I feel I'm suitably qualified to be your guide.)

If you have never started your own business, don't discount the chapters that appear to be targeted at the entrepreneur or business owner. Greater minds than mine have pointed out how the era of a job for life is long over – that ship has sailed. More and more, organizations are encouraging their employees to think like entrepreneurs. Get closer to the customer. Take risks. Be passionate about projects. How else can I add value? What value *do* I add? Why do I deserve a salary rise? And so on.

What I've done is to rack my brains and come up with (what's turned out to be) 24 subjects about which I wish I'd known more when I started working. Thus, the book has 24 chapters in alphabetical order.

The book is intended to be quick and easy to read, punchy and concise. The chapters are all pretty short. I take as my starting point that you're like the rest of us – that you've got far more to do than you'll ever have time to do it. So you don't want to spend too much time messing around with this book.

While you can certainly read it from cover to cover – and would get benefit from doing that – my sense is that the most effective way to use the book would be to dip into it. You're asked to attend a meeting, for example, so you check the chapter on meetings. You're asked to take on a new project but before you start calling meetings, sending out emails, banging stuff into your computer, hiring people, making Gantt charts in Microsoft Project and so on, you take a few minutes out to read the chapter on projects.

I would pretty much guarantee that the time you spend on this book would be repaid several or even many times over by time you wouldn't waste as a result. Not a bad deal, eh?

Each chapter is short and focused on a very specific subject. The main body of each chapter talks about the issues associated with that subject. The book is very much a how-to book so it then goes on to tell you how to deal with these issues. In other words, it identifies some specific actions that you can take straight away in order to learn the lesson of the chapter.

Littered throughout the book are extracts from carefully selected commencement speeches – where the great and the good give advice to graduating university students. In commencement speeches, the speaker recounts past experiences and tries to crystallize the lessons they learned from these. Essentially, these lessons, which they are now passing on to people about to go into the workplace, are the things *they* wish they'd known when *they* started working.

So these commencement speeches fitted in very nicely with the concept of the book. While I found some of these speeches to be of questionable quality, there were also some truly great ones there. So I've taken the best of these and spread them throughout the book. I've also drawn on some of the wisdom of the great and good throughout history – from Roman times to the present day.

So will this book change your life? Well, surely the change needs to come from within. But it should certainly inspire and support change.

Is it free from fluffiness and cod-philosophy? Yes – we've tried to ensure that it is.

Does it contain useful, actionable insight? For sure – it is common sense, hopefully elucidated with uncommon clarity.

Does it allow dip-in-dip-out reading, for that quick refresher/morale boost at those times your commitment to change is wavering? It certainly does. It's written in manageable chunks, which we hope you will find enjoyable to read.

And so without further ado, let's launch into it.

AIMING HIGH

THE ONLY LIMITS ARE THE ONES YOU SET YOURSELF

At some point in any career, a normally unjustifiable risk might need to be taken to make the quantum leap from the mediocre to the big time.

– Sir Ranulph Fiennes, British explorer

remember being a kid and watching on a black and white TV the Alabama race riots. I remember – even as a kid – wondering how this problem could ever be solved, how this level of hatred could ever be overcome. Fast forward 50 years and there's a coloured president in the White House. Pretty much anything is possible.

In my teens and twenties, the Iron Curtain was a fixed part of the geography of Europe. It was hard to see how that situation could ever change. Look at the map of Europe now. Germany is reunited, democracies (of various qualities) in almost all of the countries of the former Soviet Union and that country itself a distant memory. And all of that happened in a just a handful of years. Pretty much anything is possible.

In 2000, my company numbered nearly 50 people. When the dot.com bubble burst, much of our business disappeared overnight. Thinking this was a temporary thing, we tried to ride out the storm rather than getting small quickly, which is what we should have done. Bad mistake. As a result, we ended up with a debt of – essentially – $1,000,000. Fast forward to now and we're debt free, small, profitable and thriving. I'll say it again – pretty much anything is possible.

Have you ever thought how lucky you are to have been born at this time in the history of the world?

Imagine if you had been born in the Middle Ages or indeed pretty much any time before about the middle of the nineteenth century. If you had, and unless you were lucky enough to have been born into that tiny percentage of the world's wealthy people, you would have died as you started out – a peasant or a farmer or a miner or a factory worker or a soldier or something similar.

These days, it's all different. These days, you can do whatever you want. You can become whatever you want to be. You can start out as the child of parents who do whatever for a living and you can end up doing something entirely different that has never been done by any of your family members or ancestors before you. Harold May was a draughtsman at the Ministry of Aviation – his son Brian went on to become guitarist with Queen.

If your parents are not well off, you don't have to be too – if that's what you want. In 2008, Warren Buffet, was reckoned by *Forbes* magazine to be the richest man in the world with a net worth of $62,000,000,000. Buffet was born in 1930. His father was a congressman whose salary at that time would have been $9,000 per annum.

If your family were people who didn't seek the limelight, you don't have to be like them – you can put yourself out there – all over the Internet – if you want to. Beyoncé's father worked for Xerox and her mother owned a hair salon.

Basically – you don't have to do anything anybody in your family did before – all down through history. You can go and plough your own course. The world is your oyster.

What a privilege. What a blessing.

> '*If you think you are too small to make a difference,*
> *try sleeping with a mosquito*'.
> – The Dalai Lama

And there's another thing. In my lifetime, the idea of moving up the ladder was the accepted thing. I did it myself for a time – until (you might say) I wised up. This was my ladder:

- First in mathematical physics
- Software engineer
- Project manager
- Managing a software group
- Managing a much larger software group
- Set up a subsidiary of a software company

before starting my own thing.

These days you can skip the ladder if you want. You can become the CEO of your own company in the morning, if you're so inclined. Larry Page is co-founder of Google. This was Larry's ladder:

- Bachelor of Science
- Master of Science
- Began a PhD
- Co-president of Google

How's that for jumping several rungs of the ladder rather than laboriously climbing up each one in turn?

So given that you've been born at this great time in history and granted this extraordinary opportunity, what are you going to do with it?

The answer – it seems to me – is that you need to aim high. Why shouldn't you? The opportunity is there and we're surrounded by evidence that these opportunities can be seized; any mountain climbed and any summit reached.

> *'Whether you think you can, or think you can't – you're right'.*
> – Henry Ford, founder of the Ford Motor Company

Aim high. There's no reason why you shouldn't. You just need to have confidence in yourself. There is no ceiling, no limit. Or rather, the only ceilings and limits are the ones you set yourself.

How is it that we set these ceilings? While it's easy to blame your parents, I think they may definitely have something to do with it. My father's advice to me was to 'get a good education and then get a good job'. Given where he had come from – leaving an economically depressed Ireland in the 1940s, and straight into World War II where he served in the British Merchant Navy, then returning to a post-war Britain to look for a job – this was probably good advice, as he saw it. I hope my advice to my children has been a bit closer to the mark – 'Find what you like to do and then see if you can make some money from it'.

But it's not just our parents. Sometimes we just make assumptions as to how far we can go or how high we can climb or what we can achieve. Or we slide from school or college into a job and then another (more senior, better paying) job and another and another. We take on more and more financial responsibilities – a car, a house, a partner, children – and before we know it we're far off down a path that we maybe never really intended to travel.

Perhaps – when it comes right down to it – these ceilings are just caused by thoughtlessness – not consciously thinking about or deciding what it is we want to do with the precious life of ours.

> *'Our deepest fear is not that we are inadequate. Our deepest fear is that we are powerful beyond measure. It is our light not our darkness that most frightens us. We ask ourselves, who am I to be brilliant, gorgeous, talented and fabulous? Actually, who are you not to be?'*
>
> – Marianne Williamson, spiritual teacher and author

So that's really the thing here. Think about what it is you want to do and aim high. All the later chapters in this book will then work better for you – if you take a more expansive, imaginative approach to the things you do in work and in life. Ask yourself what you would do if you won the lottery – if earning a living was no longer an issue. Ask yourself what you would do if a fairy god-mother suddenly appeared and said that you can be/do/become whatever you want.

. . . looking back, I grew up in a world of unlimited opportunity. Each night I would read, and reading opened up the world to me. I love reading history and especially biography. In biographies, you are almost always reading about people who started out unimportant but ended up having a significant life.

What I liked most about biographies then and now is that the person you are reading about is in his or her early life on page 50, doesn't know about the success he or she will achieve on page 300. They couldn't see the greatness that lay ahead. If you think about it, that's a great justification for the optimism that you should have for the life ahead of you. All of you are only on about page 50 of your biography, with hundreds of pages to go.

– Lloyd Blankfein, Goldman Sachs Chairman and CEO, LaGuardia Community College commencement speech, 6 June 2013[1]

APPRECIATING LIFE

IT'S ABOUT HOW YOU SEE THINGS

'What day is it?'
'It's today', squeaked Piglet.
'My favourite day', said Pooh.

– from *Winnie the Pooh* by A.A. Milne

Yes, we should aim high and yes, we should have goals but – almost paradoxically – we also need to live in the moment.

You don't want to suffer from When–Then Syndrome. When this happens, then I'll be happy. When I get my boss's job then I'll be happy. When I have a bestselling novel then I'll be happy. When I have enough money then I can pursue my passion. When the mortgage is paid off . . . the kids have been through college . . . etc. etc. You don't want to be in an endless pursuit of the perfect life while missing what's right there in front of you.

There's only today. So enjoy the journey. Appreciate what you have. Be grateful for the good things that have come to you. If you are, more good things will come. It's about the journey, not the destination.

I went through a period of thinking I was a failure. I wanted more than anything to be a novelist. I was writing fiction and it wasn't getting published. Failure. At last, I got an agent. And he found a publisher but then my books weren't making it onto the best-seller lists. More failure. I nearly got two movie deals over the line, one involving an A-list star – but the operative word for me was 'nearly'. Failure. Failure. Failure.

Then one day I realized – hey, I'm getting to spend more and more of my days writing. I may not be making much money from it but I'm a novelist. I'm writing novels. That was what I wanted and that's what I'm doing. Where's the failure in that?

I wised up. I realized that yes, it's important to have these goals, to aim high. But what matters more is to live in the moment,

Hope that your journey is a long one.
May there be many summer mornings when,
with what pleasure, what joy,
you come into harbors you're seeing for the first time;
may you stop at Phoenician trading stations
to buy fine things,
mother of pearl and coral, amber and ebony,
sensual perfume of every kind-
as many sensual perfumes as you can;
and may you visit many Egyptian cities
to learn and learn again from those who know.

Keep Ithaca always in your mind.
Arriving there is what you're destined for.
But don't hurry the journey at all.
Better if it lasts for years,
so that you're old by the time you reach the island,
wealthy with all you've gained on the way,
not expecting Ithaca to make you rich.
Ithaca gave you the marvelous journey.
Without her you would have not set out.
She has nothing left to give you now.

And if you find her poor, Ithaca won't have fooled you.
Wise as you will have become, so full of experience,
you'll have understood by then what these Ithacas mean.

– Extract from *Ithaca* by Constantine P. Cavafy, Greek poet. This
was inspired by the Homeric story of Odysseus returning home.
You can also hear a wonderful version of this recited by
Sir Sean Connery on YouTube.[2]

appreciate each day because ultimately, that's what our lives are – a collection of days. If you aim to spend your days happily, then – in the end – that it what matters. *That's* what success is.

If you're having difficulty with this mindset, then here are a whole bunch of things that could help:

1. Slow down, do less. Take a day out where you do the absolute bare minimum – where, rather than focusing on packing in as much as you can to the day, pack in as little as possible. Friday is my day for doing this.
2. Be present. Whatever you're doing pay attention to it. Take the earphones out if you're travelling on the train. Switch off the background music or the TV.
3. Disconnect. Spend some time – a couple of hours, an evening, a day – without your mobile phone, email, Facebook, Twitter and all the rest of that stuff.
4. Be present to people. The American philosopher Thoreau put it best: 'The greatest compliment that was ever paid me was when one asked me what I thought, and attended to my answer'.
5. Get out in nature. Go for a walk. Stroke the dog. Smell the flowers. It's a cliché I know, but how true it is.
6. Enjoy your food. Have you ever seen a child eating? If you haven't, take a proper look next time. Notice how present they are to the food – they may be smearing it all over their face but my goodness, all their senses are engaged in the activity of eating.
7. Take a different route to work. It's not just a way of getting from A to B; it's a journey with all the excitement that implies. Even if it's your daily commute that you've made a thousand times, today's is not going to be the same as yesterday's.

8. See if you can find some pleasure in anything you do. Even if it's something that wouldn't conventionally be regarded as pleasurable or even if it's something that you hate, I'd be surprised if – once you got stuck into it – you couldn't find at least one thing about it that wasn't bad.

There is no 25th hour in the day, so don't look for it. Take time. Stop. Look around you. Freeze the moment. Use your eyes and your mind to take pictures – mental pictures. Store the images like photographs in your head and your heart. If you already do that, good for you. If you don't, but think it's a good idea, it's not too late to start right now. Look around and remember this moment. At the end of the day, it's not the person with the most toys who wins – it's the person with the most memories. Because, when you're sitting in your rocking chair at the young age of 100, those memories are gonna be like old friends. Someone you can call on to make you smile. And the more of those old friends that come around, the better.

– Jon Bon Jovi, American musician, Monmouth University commencement speech, 16 May 2001[3]

BEING MORE PRODUCTIVE

WHY THE ANSWER IS NOT 16-HOUR DAYS

There is nothing so useless as doing efficiently that which should not be done at all.

— Peter Drucker, management writer and theorist

W e're all becoming busier. Do you find that:

- You're always pressed for time?
- There never seem to be enough hours in the day?
- You wake up in the morning feeling a great load on you of all the things you have to do that day?
- You are stressed in work because of overload?
- You think you've never done enough?

Imagine waking up in the morning and instead of feeling a great weight on you, asking yourself: what things do I need to put into this empty day?

Rather than stressing about how much you need to pack into the day ahead, imagine asking what actually needs to be done and why? Why do you think a certain thing is so important? If you can't come up with a good enough answer, are you going to do it anyway? And if so, why? Why would you do that?

There's an exercise I do on my training courses where I get people to figure out how much work they have to do and how much time they have available to do it. Ten or fifteen years ago it would have been really unusual to find somebody who was 100% overloaded. (Pause and think about this for a moment – 100% overloaded means doing the work of *two* people.) These days, the same exercise yields about half the people on the course being 100% *or more* overloaded. And this situation is not getting better.

Faced with workloads like this, how can people be productive? It seems to me that people adopt two strategies to deal with this situation. Let's look at them in turn.

Time management

The first thing people say is, 'Ah ha, it's a time management problem'. So they go on a course or buy a book – and then more often than not, fall back into their old ways.

If you go on a time management course or read a time management book and do what it says and, then sure, you will get more done. But you won't have solved the problem of having too much to do and not enough time to do it. That is not the problem that time management courses and books solve. So when people say, 'I fell back into my old ways', that's not what happened. It was just that the problem of too much to do and not enough time to do it hadn't gone away.

So when time management doesn't work, the next thing people try is to work crazy hours.

Working crazy hours

Now I can only assume that if somebody works crazy hours, they believe – though they may not have actually rationalized it like this – that if they work long enough hours, they will get everything done.

And I can only say that if you believe that, then you're nuts. You could work all the hours you were given and not get everything done. You could be granted several lifetimes and not get everything done.

It's also worth saying that working long hours for sustained periods of time is completely unproductive as the following table shows.

Endless long hours	Normal working hours
Got all the time in the world – 'If I don't get it done today, there's always tomorrow'	Have to get certain things done today
No life outside work	A life outside work
Often no clear goal or plan other than to work long hours	Very clear goal and a plan to get there
No differentiation between important and unimportant things – 'I'll get to it eventually'	Focus on the important things
Constant time wasting	Very little time wasting
Physically unhealthy	Physically healthy
A sense of trying to clear a vast mountain of stuff	A sense of definite and consistent progress towards an end goal
Potentially very stressful	Low stress

'Working ten-hour days allows you to fall behind twice as fast as you could working five hour days'.
– Isaac Asimov, American author

But there is a solution to being more productive. And – bizarrely – that solution is instead of trying to do *more,* we should be trying to do *less.*

Now in some ways, this is a very radical idea. But in other ways it's not radical at all. Since – clearly – some things will never be done, it's just a question of who decides. You can let Fate decide – by which I mean a combination of the culture of the organization in which you work, your own culture, your boss's personality, the guilt you feel when leaving on time, random things that happen during the day and a whole bunch of others factors – or you can decide. All I'm proposing here is that you decide.

Do less

Here's how to do it. (I know there are issues here about who can make these decisions but for the moment, you make them. You decide. Then, we'll talk about who else has to get involved.)

1. Make a list of everything you have to do in work.
2. Now divide the list into the things that are wildly important and the things that aren't. And no, not everything is 'wildly' important:

First, you decide – as though the decision rested completely with you.

It doesn't, of course – so now check it with whoever you have to check it with – most likely your boss.

Finally, if there are things on your list that your boss thinks are important but you're not convinced, then test your theory. Don't do them and see what happens. (I'm quite serious about this.) You'll soon find out! There's some more detail on each of these below.

3. For the things that are wildly important, prioritize them. Do this by taking the list and asking, 'If I could only do one thing, what would it be?' This becomes your #1 priority. Now take the remaining list and ask the question again – 'If I could only do one thing, what would it be?' This is your #2 priority. Keep doing this until the list is prioritized.

4. For the things that are not wildly important, ignore them. Don't do them. Ever.

Which brings me to my last word of advice – value. There is a horrible modern phenomenon that I am going to beg all of you not to fall prey to – multi-tasking.

It may seem like you're being more productive, excelling at time management, and impressively dexterous – texting, tweeting, listening to a commencement speech – all at the same time.

But, I'm convinced as a society we're more anxious and stressed because we're trying to do too much at once – and in doing so end up doing none of it as well as we could. So, I'm going to champion single-tasking.

Focusing your mind, time and energy – to bring the full value of what you have to offer to the task at hand, to your passions, your family, and your community. To be fully present in all your endeavors. To make courageous choices – deciding in the face of competing demands where you will get and give the most value.

– Barbara Desoer, President of Home Loans, Bank of America, UC Berkeley Haas School of Business commencement speech, 15 May 2011[4]

Keep it going

If you like the sound of this idea, then you could start tomorrow – behaving as though this were true. But here's how to keep it going long-term and make it part of the way you work. There are five things you can do.

1 Get buy-in

You're probably going to have to get buy-in from other people, most notably from your boss. The way to do it is to use the inescapable logic of this chapter and a few facts. You need to show your boss how overloaded you are. Email me and I'll send you a fill-in-the-blanks spreadsheet for doing exactly that. Now go to your boss and show him these numbers. Explain that with this level of overload, the dead hand of Fate will be operating:

- Some things won't get done at all.
- Some things will be delayed or run late.
- You'll work longer hours which will just reduce your productivity.
- And – with the best will in the world – some things will be done less than well or incompletely.

Then propose the solution. Why don't we (you and I, boss) decide what's going to be done rather than letting Fate decide?

2 Make sure the things you have to do are measurable – not vague

You need to make sure that everything in your 'Wildly Important' list is measureable. For example, 'Reach a sales target of €/£/$ 35K per month' is measureable; 'Increase sales' is not. Do this by agreeing with your boss what the measures are going to be.

One you've done this, you've got a deal – 'The Deal'.

3 Live the deal

If something comes to you and it's one of your wildly important things, give it time, energy, commitment, knowledge, experience, passion, love, even – all that good stuff you're capable of.

If something comes to you that's not wildly important, don't do it. Why on earth would you? It doesn't contribute towards your measured goal. It therefore has no real value and should not be done.

If your boss (or anyone else) complains about this, say, 'We had a deal'. (The deal can be renegotiated but once it's agreed, then you – and your boss – have to live the deal. You need to be a bit hard assed about this, if necessary. Your boss will very quickly toe the line.)

4 Test the deal

In some ways, the most cunning bit of all of this. It's especially for those people who thought that everything they do is wildly important.

There will be things on your 'Wildly Important' list which could never possibly end up on the not-wildly-important side. But there may be some things that you're not convinced about. These are the things near the bottom of your 'Wildly Important' priority list. Your boss says they're important but you're not sure they are.

So you're going to test them. How will you do this? Simple. Don't do them and see what happens.

One of two things will happen. Either the sky will fall – because the thing was wildly important after all – or it won't. If the sky falls, you have your answer. But if the sky doesn't fall, then first of all, you've saved a little piece of your precious time. But now, more importantly, you've set a precedent. If this thing wasn't done once, it could not be done again. And over time, something which supposedly was wildly important could end up on the not-wildly-important side.

I've come across countless examples of this.

For instance, I've had many, many people tell me about meetings they stopped going to and nothing bad happened as a result.

And people who found a better, more streamlined way to do something that replaced an established, clunky way. The more streamlined way stayed on their 'Wildly Important' list and the more clunky one was consigned to the not-wildly-important side.

5 Say 'no' nicely

When something comes to you that's not wildly important, it will continue to torment you unless you say 'no' nicely to it.

It's easy to find ways to say 'no' nicely. Sit down for 10 minutes and you could come up with at least 10. (Try it.) Get with a friend or loved one, pour yourselves a glass of wine or a beer, and you could come up with 10 more – 5 that you could use in work and 5 in your domestic life. (Try that – it can be a blast.) In my book, *The Power of Doing Less*[5] there's a whole chapter on saying 'no' nicely.

In conclusion, it's possible to be more productive but paradoxically the thing is not to do more. That's a mug's game that you have no chance of winning.

Try doing less for a while and see how you go. Decide what you're going to invest your previous time into and what you're not. Don't let outside forces do it for you. When faced with a 'why should I put my time into this?' decision, if you can't come up with a good enough answer, then you need to pass on it.

Finally, here are a pair of quotes from Tim Ferriss, author of the hugely successful *The 4-Hour Work Week*.[6]

> 'Decision *is* related to the word incision, it means "to cut off". It means to cut away other options and to commit and to focus'.
>
> 'I've interviewed everyone from gold medalists to CEOs who make $100 million a year, and their one common characteristic is the ability to "single-task" without interruption'.

Really take the two of these on board and they would transform your life.

BOSSES

WHAT THEY'RE LIKE AND WHAT THEY LIKE

If you think your boss is stupid, remember: you wouldn't have a job if he was any smarter.

– John Gotti, American mobster

While there must almost certainly be exceptions, most bosses aren't psychos. I've met quite a few bosses in my time and though I'm no psychotherapist, as far as I could tell, none of them were psychos. Most of them seemed to be just regular guys and gals like you and me, trying to do their best in the world – do a decent job, earn a crust, love the people they should love and have some fun.

That having been said though, there are some things about bosses you need to know. The first one is their greatest weakness.

Bosses make mistakes – 'OMG there's a surprise'

The greatest weakness bosses have is that they are human – just like you and me. (I know some of you reading this now may disagree with this statement but it is actually factually true.) As a result of this terrible failing they make mistakes. I've been a boss for over 35 years and have made literally countless mistakes. You would like to think, of course, that as I get more experience at being a boss I would make fewer mistakes. Indeed I would like to think that myself.

The trouble is that it may not actually be true.

The things I do now – that I do because of the experience I've gained and the mistakes that I've made – may not actually be the right things or the best things for today's world. At least not all of them. And so – which are and which aren't? Hell if I know!

If we then assume that your boss is no different from me – he or she also makes mistakes – then the first thing you need to be aware of is that he or she will not always be right. Let me just say that again in case you missed it.

Your boss is not always right.

This means that when your boss does something you think is wrong or makes a decision that you think is faulty or asks you to do something which you think is stupid, you need to believe in yourself and point this out.

Now before you rush into anything here, let me say that there are plenty of ways for you *not* to do this. Asking your boss publicly, say, at a meeting with a large number of attendees including *his* boss, the question, 'How could you have been so stupid, you tosser?' would be one such way. Or sending an email with the title line 'You damn idiot' would be another.

The only way to point out to your boss that he or she has made a mistake – and to survive the encounter – is to use facts.

For example, if you know that 10 widgets can be processed in a day, then 100 widgets will take 2 weeks, *provided you have nothing else to do.* If your boss then insists that you do that great favourite of bosses – multitasking, that is spread yourself across one or more other things – and still get your 100 widgets done in 2 weeks, you need to point out – using these facts – that what your boss is proposing is not a runner. In short – this dog won't hunt.

A variation on this is to use logic or rather get your boss to explain their logic. 'Why is this a good idea?' 'Tell me the thinking behind this'. Getting them to think or talk it through may get them to see the error of their ways.

At several points in the history of my company, we hired a CEO to replace me. (Some of these experiences were happier than others.) I remember one CEO explaining to me how he had assessed the salaries everyone was on and he reckoned that one salary was way out of line with everyone else's. He was therefore proposing to reduce that person's salary. Because the person in question was quite mild-mannered, the CEO reckoned this wouldn't be a problem – the person would just happily accept this action.

'You might have a think', I suggested, 'about what you would do if I did that to you?'

The matter never came up again.

> *'I don't want any yes-men around me. I want everyone to tell me the truth – even if it costs him his job'.*
>
> – Sam Goldwyn, American film producer

Bosses like to have their problems solved

Some bosses are fond of the saying, 'Don't bring me problems, bring me solutions'. I don't like that expression and would never use it myself, but there is a certain truth in it. If you can solve my problem, perhaps not in the way that I would have liked it solved, but in some way, then that's a hell of a lot better than just saying, 'Nope, can't do that'.

So coming back to our 100 widgets problem again, you could offer me alternatives. For instance:

- 'I can do the 100 in 2 weeks provided I have nothing else to do.'
- Or – even better – 'I can do the 100 in 2 weeks provided I have nothing else to do. So could Charlie take my other stuff? I checked with him and he has some bandwidth at the moment'.
- Or – 'I can do the 100 widgets *and* get this other stuff done but then that's going to take 4 weeks'.

Another example of this would be if you are overloaded and you want to do something about it. If you just go to your boss and say, 'I'm overloaded, boss', here's what's likely to happen. Your boss will put his arm around your shoulders and say, 'You think you're overloaded? You should see my schedule'.

This is a pointless discussion.

But if you go to your boss and say, 'I'm overloaded but here are some ways that the overload could be reduced/fixed – give this job to Charlie, delay that other project, get me some help with this other things', you're far more likely to get some positive action.

Bosses have a tendency to be delusional

The fact that bosses are human can't really be helped. However, what *can* be helped is the fact that many bosses – and I stress the 'many' – have a tendency to be delusional.

Here's the most obvious example I've come across. If you have ever heard a boss say, 'This is a very aggressive target/schedule/

deadline', then – in my experience, they have already parted company with reality and are living in a strange and dangerous place.

Watch out for phrases like 'stretch goals', 'ambitious targets', 'BHAGs' (Big Hairy Audacious Goals).

Let me be clear. I have no problem with ambitious goals. I'm a great man for them myself. Our reach *should* exceed our grasp. But there's a difference between ambitious goals and losing the plot. Too many bosses lose the plot.

Once again, the only way to treat a delusional boss is with facts. Every other way is pretty much guaranteed to fail. If the basis of the negotiation is that they're senior and you're junior, you'll fail. They'll just order you to do it – to charge that machine gun. If the basis of the negotiation is that they're aggressive/assertive/maybe even something of a bully, you'll fail. If the basis of the negotiation is that it's a personality clash, that is, basically you don't like each other, then you'll fail. If the basis of the negotiation is that they have money that you want, for example you're looking for a raise, then you'll fail.

But if the basis of the negotiation is the facts that you're presenting, then this is the one area where you can't fail. This is the one area where you have authority, where your knowledge is superior. Use it. Don't be a victim.

And just in case you're wondering – I've been preaching this message for 20 odd years and the following has never happened to me. Nobody has ever phoned me up and said, 'I lost my bloody job as a result of your stupid advice'.

Bosses like long hours

The other big flaw that many bosses tend to have is that they equate attendance with productivity. In other words, they confuse being at work/in the office/working long hours with being a good employee.

This is just nonsense.

Productivity is getting stuff done, achieving certain goals or targets.

Attendance is being at the office – clocking in early and clocking out late.

Once again, the way to deal with these bosses is with facts. Agree – at the beginning of the year or whenever – what your targets are. Now – *and this is utterly vital* – agree how those targets will be measured. Without measures you have no way of knowing whether you've succeeded or not. Once you've done that, work the hours required to meet the targets and meet (or better still, exceed) the measures. If anyone complains about your hours – including your boss – point them at your achievements.

I often ask a class of managers, 'Who in here gets too much feedback?' Hands rarely, if ever, go up. In fact, my experience is that employees at all levels are starving for feedback. They have bosses who say, 'If you don't hear from me, assume you're doing a good job'. That's asking people to accept neglect as a compliment. Or 'I don't praise people for doing what they're supposed to'. And we wonder why some organizations struggle with employee engagement.

– Jill Geisler, Head of The Poynter Institute's Leadership and Management programs, Duquesne University School of Leadership and Professional Advancement commencement speech, 9 August 2012[7]

COMMITMENT AND PERSEVERANCE

ONE GETS YOU STARTED, THE OTHER KEEPS YOU GOING

The three great essentials to achieve anything worthwhile are: Hard work, Stick-to-itiveness and Common sense.

– Thomas Edison, American inventor

When I was four my mum read *Treasure Island* to me and I'm pretty sure that's when I decided I wanted to be a novelist. Not that I would have understood any of that at the time. All I knew was that some power had whisked me away from an ordinary suburban childhood to a place that was exciting and scary and filled with the most amazing characters. Later I would realize that this was what novels did and that I wanted to be able to do that – create and live in these alternative worlds.

During my teens I wrote a little – mainly rambling, introspective pieces that were mainly about girls – why I loved them, why they didn't love me, how I could get to love them and so on and so on. You know the kind of thing.

I wrote a few little stories. But the big one – a novel – well, I never went anywhere near that. I was afraid to try. What if what I wrote was no good? What if I wrote a few pages and then dried up? There was no way I could stretch those flimsy ideas of mine out to 300 pages or more. And the notion that anyone would read, let alone buy, something I wrote seemed too unlikely for words.

But one day – I can't even remember it now – one day in my late twenties, the spell was broken. For some reason – I don't know what it was – I started a novel. I wrote a page or two. And then a day or two later I wrote some more. And after that some more. And more. And eventually I ended up writing a novel.

It was rejected by every publisher that I sent it to – and I sent it to a lot.

It's good that it was. It was very bad.

Of course I didn't realize how bad it was at the time. And so I kept on sending it. And they kept on rejecting it. But more importantly, while all of this was going on, I started another one.

Starting was much easier this second time and the idea and the plot – I still think – were pretty good and original. However, the characterization was fairly poor with the characters wooden and clichéd. But I finished it. An agent in the United States nearly took it on but then she suddenly stopped calling. And I continued to bolster the profits of the postal service by sending it out to publishers and agents and they continued to send back the rejections. (It would not be an exaggeration to say that I could literally paper several rooms of an average suburban house with the rejection letters I have received over the years.) But, in what was becoming a bit of a familiar ritual now, I started on a third one.

This one took me 10 years. It wasn't full time, you understand – I had a day job. And this one was good. I knew that as I was writing it. Part of the reason it was good was that it took me 10 drafts to get it right. If a particular piece didn't deliver the emotional impact I was looking for I threw it away and tried again, trying to up my game each time. This was novel writing in a different league from what I had done previously. But if I hadn't played in the previous leagues, I wouldn't have known what it was to play in this league.

Once I was finished I started the sending out again. Once again there were lots of rejections but this time, one publisher said yes. (And often – in many areas of endeavour – all it takes is one.)

Soon proofs were coming to be corrected and there was a cover design to sign off on. And then one day a package arrived at my house. In it were 10 copies. I held one in my hand. I remember thinking what a small object it was to have resulted from such a huge amount of work. The book was really well received. One reviewer described it as 'better than *Schindler's List*' – which itself had won the Booker Prize. My book was nominated for two prizes.

> *'It does not matter how slowly you go as long as you do not stop'.*
>
> – Confucius, Chinese philosopher

My fifth novel was published on 21 June 2014. I'm a novelist. Nelson Mandela said it would be like this. He said, 'It always seems impossible until it's done'.

The thing you've got to understand is that I don't think it's talent that has gotten me to this point. Sure, I have some talent but so do many people. Nor is it passion – and I'm *very* passionate about writing fiction. No – I believe it's two other things entirely.

Those two things are commitment and perseverance. Commitment got me started; perseverance kept me going.

Listen to me carefully. I can't say this clearly enough.

Whatever you want to do – you can do it. All you need is these two companions on your journey – commitment to get you started, perseverance to keep you going.

Commitment

> *'A journey of a thousand miles begins*
> *with a single step'.*
> – Lao-Tzu, Chinese philosopher

J.K. Rowling showed commitment during the seven years she took to write the first *Harry Potter* book. She was going through a divorce and living with her daughter in a tiny flat, subsisting on state benefits. Her manuscript was rejected by 12 publishers before finally being accepted. (I often wonder what those publishers think about now when they lie awake in the small hours of the night.)

The Beatles showed commitment when they were told that 'guitar groups are on the way out' and that they had 'no future in show business'.

The thing about commitment – and I've experienced this time and time again in my own life – is that once you commit, once you cross that bridge or burn those boats, then all sorts of unexpected things happen. Opportunities emerge, doors open, people appear. Others have also noted this same phenomenon.

In the nineteenth century, the American philosopher, Henry David Thoreau, talked about commitment in his famous book, *Walden*: 'if one advances confidently in the direction of his dreams, and endeavors to live the life which he has imagined, he will meet with a success unexpected in common hours. He will put some things behind, will pass an invisible boundary; new, universal, and more liberal laws will begin to establish themselves around and within him; or the old laws will be expanded, and interpreted in his favor in a more liberal sense, and he will live with the license of a higher order of beings . . . if you have built castles in the air, your work need not be lost; that is where they should be. Now put the foundations under them'.

And last century, the Scottish mountaineer, William Hutchison Murray, said it in his 1951 book, *The Scottish Himalayan Expedition*:[8] 'but when I said that nothing had been done I erred in one important matter. We had definitely committed ourselves and were halfway out of our ruts. We had put down our passage money – booked a sailing to Bombay. This may sound too simple, but is great in consequence. Until one is committed, there is hesitancy, the chance to draw back, always ineffectiveness. Concerning all acts of initiative (and creation), there is one elementary truth, the ignorance of which kills countless ideas and splendid plans: that the moment one definitely commits oneself, then Providence moves too. All sorts of things occur to help one that would never otherwise have occurred. A whole stream of events issues from the decision, raising in one's favour all manner of unforeseen incidents and meetings and material assistance, which no man could have dreamt would have come his way. I learned a deep respect for one of Goethe's couplets:

> *'Whatever you can do or dream you can, begin it.*
> *Boldness has genius, power and magic in it!'*

In some ways, commitment is the easiest thing in the world. All you have to do is take that first step. Perseverance will take care of the rest.

Perseverance

> 'The man who moves a mountain begins by carrying
> away small stones'.
>
> – Confucius, Chinese philosopher

Confucius hit the nail on the head there. This is how everything gets done.

Look at what Walt Disney went on to do. This is the same Walt Disney who was fired from the *Kansas City Star* newspaper because he was told that he lacked creativity. (By a funny coincidence, that's also something one of my former bosses once told me!) There is a story that Disney was turned down *302 times* before he finally got the financing to create Disney World.

Think of anyone who is described as 'an overnight success'. It's almost certain that when you look a little more closely, they've been grafting away for years. Most of us have seen Susan Boyle's audition on *Britain's Got Talent* – the audition that catapulted her to overnight success.

Susan Boyle began singing in school productions at age 12, and she and her mother often talked about her possibly becoming famous. Boyle sang for years in pubs and local competitions before *Britain's Got Talent.* She worked and grafted away for a long time; there was nothing overnight about it.

So when you falter and you feel like giving up, then Thomas Edison is there to whisper in your ear that 'Many of life's failures are people who did not realize how close they were to success when they gave up.' (I had figured this part out for myself. A favourite saying of mine is that. 'There has to be another way'.)

And if the going really gets tough then there is no better man to have at your side than the redoubtable Winston Churchill who'll advise you that 'If you are going through hell, keep going'.

Play the long game. Just keep showing up. Just keep taking that next step. That's not too difficult, is it?

> *Nothing in the world can take the place of persistence. Talent will not; nothing is more common than unsuccessful men with talent. Genius will not; unrewarded genius is almost a proverb. Education will not; the world is full of educated derelicts. Persistence and determination are omnipotent. The slogan 'press on' has solved and always will solve the problems of the human race.*
>
> – Calvin Coolidge, 30th President of the United States

COMMON SENSE

IT'S NOT ALL THAT COMMON BUT IT'S A SKILL YOU CAN LEARN

Common Sense is genius dressed in its working clothes.

— Ralph Waldo Emerson, American essayist and poet

'The trouble with common sense', the old saw goes, 'is that it's not all that common'. And in my experience, nowhere is this truer than in work or business where I have seen very, very smart people – far smarter than I'll ever be – propose or do some incredibly dumb things.

Of course it's easy to say that someone doesn't have much common sense. It's such a vague statement that it could mean almost anything. So a few years back I decided to try and codify common sense. I would write a book that identified the 'principles' (if that's not too grand a word – though I think it probably is) of common sense. More simply, the book would identify a bunch of things which if you were doing them or even conscious of them, then you would be exhibiting common sense.

The result was a book called *Simply Brilliant*.[9] The book sold pretty well. In fact I think I'm correct in saying that it's been my best seller to date and with the most translations.

Common sense is a skill. It can be learned.

And why would this be a good thing to do? Well – a couple of reasons. The first and most important one is that it gives you a framework for thinking, a sort of mental checklist. If, for example, somebody is proposing a certain course of action or project or venture, you can run it by your mental checklist and see if it stands up.

The other reason is that you would stand out from the crowd. In my experience, not a lot of people carry around this mental checklist with them.

So here then are the 'principles' of common sense.

1 Many things are simple

Of course, some things are definitely not simple. Launching, manning and maintaining the International Space Station, for example, surely has some tremendously complex elements to it. But most of us aren't NASA engineers and scientists and a lot of the stuff we do probably has a simple explanation or solution. So if you find yourself at a meeting, for example, and the participants are working up some tremendously complex solution to a problem – chances are they're barking up the wrong tree.

The thing to do then would be to call stop. Ask if there's not a simpler solution. Ask the question, 'What would be the simplest solution to this?' or 'Can we find a simpler solution to this?' There's a good chance you'll be able to.

2 Know what you're trying to do

> 'If one does not know to which port one is sailing, no wind is favourable'.
>
> – Seneca, Roman philosopher

You need to know what you're trying to do. And you need to know *precisely* – it can't be vague.

This may sound ridiculously obvious but it's actually been the cause of death of a million projects. One of the more spectacular examples recently was the BBC's Digital Media Initiative (DMI) project cancelled in the middle of 2013 after a spend of £125.9 million.

The National Audit Office's report on the project said, among other things, that *'The BBC did not establish clear requirements'*. [My italics.]

After the cancellation, James Purnell, the BBC's director of strategy and digital, said: 'In the future we are going to rely far more on off-the-shelf technology. We've messed up and we apologize to licence fee payers for that'.

Ah – that's okay, then.

Another way of thinking about this is with the idea of 'boxes and clouds'. What you're trying to do has to be a box. It has to be well defined. You have to know what's inside the box and what's not. What are you to achieve (in the box) and what are you not trying to achieve (outside the box)?

If you don't have a box you'll have a cloud. You have no real idea what exactly you're trying to do. If you don't know then neither will other people. Such a situation is *guaranteed* to end in tears.

3 There is always a sequence of events

This is how everything gets done. Knowing the sequence of events in advance is called a plan. Knowing them while you're engaged in figuring them out is called firefighting. Knowing them after the fact is called a post-mortem.

I hope you'd agree that firefighting is dumb. I hope you'd further agree that trying to figure out what happened after everything has fallen apart is completely dumb. That leaves planning as the only option left standing.

If you want to plan anything, if you want to estimate the time something is going to take, the number of people you need, the cost or budget – you need to figure out the sequence of events.

There's more on this in the chapter called *Projects and Getting Stuff Done.*

4 Things don't get done if people don't do them

I know this sounds *ludicrously* obvious but there are a vast number of (especially) bosses out there who believe that work *can* be done without people. These are the bosses who say things like 'That's just the culture here' or 'I don't want to hear anybody using the word "can't"' or 'We like a can-do attitude here' or 'You're going to have to learn to do more with less' or 'You should be working smarter not harder' (whatever that's supposed to mean) or 'You're being inflexible' or 'You're not being a team player' or 'Is this plan based on a five-day week?' or 'You're lucky to have a job' or 'JFDI' (Just ******* Do It) or 'We have no choice – we have to do it' or 'That's not the kind of attitude we want around here' or 'I don't think you're suited to the culture of this organization'. In short – there have to be people to do the work or else the work can't be done.

5 Things rarely turn out as expected

Think about Murphy's law: 'Anything that can go wrong will go wrong'. Check out http://en.wikipedia.org/wiki/Murphy's_law if you're in any doubt about that statement. The upshot of this is that you need to consider all the possibilities before taking action.

In 1920 the United States enacted prohibition laws to suppress the alcohol trade. It was felt that this would be good both for the nation's health and for public morals. Put more simply, there would be fewer men drinking their wages, fewer drunken men beating their wives and neglecting or abusing their families.

On the face of it, it might have seemed like a good idea. Certainly, American legislators and temperance crusaders thought so.

The result, of course, was that many small-scale producers of alcohol – wineries, brewers, distillers – immediately went out of business. And if that wasn't bad enough, large-scale organized crime set up a vast illegal alcohol industry.

Things rarely turn out as expected.

And so you need to have contingency in your plans.

You also need to do a risk assessment. This is just a fancy way of saying that you need to do the following:

- Make a list of all the things you can think of that could go wrong with the venture you're proposing to undertake. These are the risks to your project.
- Grade each of these things as to their likelihood, that is, how likely they are to happen. Use a scale of 1–3. 1 is low, 3 is high, 2 in the middle.
- Grade them again as to their impact – the effect if they do happen. Use the same 1–3 scale. 1 is low, 3 is high, 2 in the middle.

- Now multiply the likelihood by the impact. For any items that end up rated a 6 or a 9, identify some actions you can take to reduce or eliminate these risks.

6 Things either are or they aren't

The cause of a million project failures. The terrifying 'we're 90% done' syndrome – which generally means that 90% of the time has gone rather than that 90% of the thing has been done. Something is either done – or it's not.

Break the project or venture down into the sequence of events – essentially, the list of jobs to be done.

Now the way to track progress is that each job can exist in only one of two states. It's either done (and hence you've made some progress) or it's not done (and so you haven't made that progress).

7 Look at things from others' points of view

The so-called 'Golden Rule' – 'Do as you would be done to'. Look on Wikipedia and prepare to be astonished by the number of civilizations and religions that this has been, and still is, a part of.

In all your working life you'll have to deal with people. Sometimes you may have difficult decisions to make that are going to affect people. You may have a bewildering variety of choices open to you – possible paths that you could take. In those circumstances it can be very enlightening to put yourself in the shoes of these other people. How will they view each choice that you might make? And in turn, how will this affect your decision making?

> *The heart of the question is whether all Americans are to be afforded equal rights and equal opportunities,* whether we are going to treat our fellow Americans as we want to be treated *[my italics]. If an American, because his skin is dark, cannot eat lunch in a restaurant open to the public, if he cannot send his children to the best public school available, if he cannot vote for the public officials who will represent him, if, in short, he cannot enjoy the full and free life which all of us want,* then who among us would be content to have the color of his skin changed and stand in his place *[my italics]? Who among us would then be content with the counsels of patience and delay?'*
>
> US President, John F. Kennedy, invoked the Golden Rule in a famous civil rights speech delivered on 11 June 1963.[10]

So there it is. Common sense. Try looking at your job/work through this lens for a few weeks and see what happens.

COMMUNICATION

YOU GOTTA KEEP 'EM IN THE LOOP

The single biggest problem in communication is the illusion that it has taken place.

– George Bernard Shaw, Irish playwright

The story of the race to see who would be the first person to stand at the South Pole at the beginning of the twentieth century is absolutely thrilling. Even if you have no interest in travel or history or exploration, I'd really recommend that get your hands on Roland Huntford's *The Last Place on Earth*.[11]

Huntford's book describes the contest between the British explorer, Robert Scott, and the Norwegian, Roald Amundsen, to be first at the South Pole. It's a fascinating story, not least because it's about two teams carrying out the same project and achieving drastically different results – one team succeeding in reaching the South Pole and getting back safely, the other failing.

One of the ways that the two expeditions were managed very differently was in the area of communication. Indeed it wouldn't be an exaggeration to say that communication was probably the key reason why one expedition was so dramatically successful and the other such a complete catastrophe.

Amundsen had a simple plan which he wrote out and then shared with all his team. He did this early in the project – while they were still on their voyage from Norway to Antarctica. His colleagues could study the plan, get to know it, make suggestions, offer improvements.

Scott, by comparison, had a plan in his head, which he really didn't share with anybody except on a need-to-know basis. His view seems to have been that since he was the leader, the plan was his – to build and to guard.

Scott changed the plan numerous times. One of the results of this was that his team were unclear about when exactly he would be returning from the South Pole. The result of this – a disastrous one, as it turned out – was that they were unsure if he was running late and whether a rescue expedition needed to be mounted. In the end, the rescue expedition was launched too late and Scott's expedition ended in disaster.

There's a message there for all of us.

> 'Tell me and I'll forget; show me and I may remember; involve me and I'll understand'.
> – Chinese proverb

If I asked you the question, 'What constitutes a successful project?' what would you say? 'Hits the deadline'. 'Comes in within the budget'. 'Meets the requirements of the customer'.

Sure – these are all aspects of a successful project, but if you want it in two words, a successful project is 'happy stakeholders'. To explain:

The stakeholders are the people who have a stake in the project. More precisely, they're the individuals or groups of people who are affected by the project in some way. Every stakeholder has 'win conditions', that is, what the stakeholder would regard as the best possible outcome to the project. To get happy stakeholders you have to deliver the win conditions.

The key to doing this is communication.

Make sure you communicate at the beginning of the project

You have to:

- Find out who the stakeholders are.
- Ask them what their win conditions are. (Don't assume that you know or that they're the same for every stakeholder.)
- Get it in writing.

You may discover that not all win conditions are achievable. For example, for the budget you're giving us, we're not going to be able to deliver that particular win condition. Or, with this number of people on our team, that target date simply isn't achievable. Then you need to communicate these facts to the stakeholders. You can't tell them lies. You can't commit to doing things you know aren't possible.

Make sure you communicate throughout the project

Once you've made an agreement with the stakeholders about what is and is not going to be done, you need to keep them in the loop. You need to tell them how things are going. Are you making progress towards their win conditions? Are you making the progress you expected? If you are, that's great. If not and there's a bad surprise looming, you need to tell them. Then they can do something about it.

Maybe you know the Dilbert cartoons – about life in the office. I have a little book of such cartoons called *Telling It Like It Isn't*.[12] In one of them, they're having a meeting – Dilbert, his boss and his colleagues.

The boss says, 'Let's go round the table and give an update on each of our projects'. It's the start of every project status meeting you've ever been at.

Dilbert says, 'My project is a pathetic series of poorly planned, near random acts'.

The boss then says, 'It's more or less customary to say that things are going fine'.

And it *is* more or less customary to say that things are going fine. You don't want to fall into that trap. If there's bad news, you've got to come out with your hands up. It won't be easy but the alternative – waiting until they find out – is no alternative at all. Forewarned, the stakeholders can do something about it. If your objective is happy stakeholders, you can't dump them in it.

A project could go badly wrong and you might still be able to recover happy stakeholders from the wreckage, if you handle them properly. Obviously they wouldn't be whoopee-doo happy but you might be able to have them saying, 'Well, that was pretty awful and we'd never want to do that again. But let's learn from our mistakes now and push on'.

And the key to handling them properly is communication. We could all do a whole lot more and it wouldn't hurt a bit.

Make sure you communicate the right thing
Finally, when you are communicating, whether face to face, by phone or by email or any other way – say what it is you want the

other party to do. Too often – and this is particularly true of email – we're just moving information around. How many times have you cc'd something to somebody? Why did you do that? What did you want them to do with the information you sent them? Should you, in fact, have cc'd them at all?

Say what it is you want.

Do you want them to take some action(s)? If so, then say what it is you want them to do.

If there's nothing you want them to do other than be aware of the information, then say that – and say it early on, so that they realize it. This may well stop them wasting time on something that isn't particularly high priority.

And if there's nothing at all you want them to do, then why are you wasting time communicating with them anyway? You want to socialize with them? No problem. Go socialize – I'm all for socializing at work. But be clear to yourself that that's what you're doing.

In conclusion, there is an old story of two bricklayers who are asked what they are doing.

One says, 'I'm building a wall'.

The second one says, 'I'm building a cathedral'.

Communication is about everybody – bosses, colleagues, peers, your team, whoever is involved in the undertaking – seeing the big picture and their part in it.

This was perhaps the key way that Amundsen was very different from Scott.

A different view on communication can be found in a commencement speech by Maria Shriver.[13] It's called 'The Power of the Pause'.

I'll leave you with a short extract:

Pausing allows you to take a beat – to take a breath in your life. As everybody else is rushing around like a lunatic out there, I dare you to do the opposite . . . it's really important to pause along the way and take a break from communicating outwardly, so you can communicate inwardly, with yourself.

Maria Shriver, American journalist, USC Annenberg School of Communication commencement speech, 11 May 2012

CREATIVITY

IT'S NOT JUST FOR ARTISTS

Find what you love and let it kill you.

— James Rhodes, British classical pianist

T he quote at the top of this chapter is taken from what may be the greatest piece of inspirational writing I have ever read.[14]

There are certain things that are meant to separate us human beings from the animals. Some of them are not very attractive – the fact that we're capable of genocide, for instance – mass killing of our own species. But that's not really what I'm thinking about here. Rather, it's the more positive things.

More specifically, I'm pretty sure that one thing that separates us from animals is our need to be creative. Now let's be clear here – I'm talking about creative in the widest possible sense of the word. It may well be that you *are* the greatest artist since Rembrandt's wife asked Rembrandt, 'Who's going to pay for the dog?'* And if you are – congratulations on having been born with such a prodigious talent. I hope you use it wisely and make the world a happier and more beautiful place.

Most of us are less blessed but all of us are given talents and all of us have a need to create. Whether that's pulling off an incredible save in Thursday night's five-a-side or clocking under three and a half hours in a marathon or cooking a gorgeous meal or painting or writing or playing music or creating a company out of nothing**

....

Obscure, I know. The reference is to Rembrandt's great work, The Night Watch *– a vast painting, 12 by 14 feet, that contains 34 characters and a dog. Each of the characters paid 100 guilders to be in the painting. It's not known who picked up the tab for the dog or if it was a stray.*

**Be careful about this one. Coming up with an idea that enables you to build a company from nothing is certainly creative. Spending 16 hours every day, years on end, at that company's office, is not.*

or building an organic garden from a patch of builder's rubble out the back. Whatever.

When you start work you want to do a good job. You want to be part of the team. Presumably something about the culture of the organization attracted you there in the first place. You want to fit in.

The trouble is that sometimes we're prepared to do whatever it takes to fit in. And that often involves giving up things that are important to us – family, hobbies, 'a life' – so that we can work.

The simple message of this chapter is to warn you against that.

I don't need to tell you how important it is for you to spend time with the man/woman you love, to watch your kids grow up, to be part of your loved ones' lives.

But I think I *do* need to tell you about creativity. In short – you need to do something creative in your life and not let anything take that away from you – not job, not family, not anything. Being creative is our highest form of self-actualization, our highest need, our greatest calling.

More than perhaps anything else, this is something *I* wish I had known when I started working.

Yes, you're going to have to earn a living, pay the mortgage and all that stuff. But don't let that be all that you do. Don't just do that, get something to eat and then crash in front of the telly for the rest of the night. Create something. A book, a painting, a meal, a (more) beautiful body, music, a comedy routine, a role in a play, a movie, the perfect game of whatever sport you play or do, a loaf of bread, a cake, a dance, clothes . . . something.

If you don't have this in your life, there will be something missing. You will wake up each day and something won't feel quite right. There will be some hunger you're not satisfying, some pull that you're not responding to, some emptiness that you feel is there.

> *'If you deliberately set out to be less than you are capable, you'll be unhappy for the rest of your life'.*
> – Abraham Maslow

If you don't have something creative in your life right now, I can pretty much guarantee that you'll be feeling what I'm describing. Your life will be incomplete in some unarticulated way.

And if you'd been wondering what that funny restlessness was that you were feeling, then that's what it is.

So you know what to do.

Satisfy the hunger. Go with the pull. Fill that void.

Your life will be the richer for it.

And, of course, far greater minds than mine have said the same thing. One is the late, great Kurt Vonnegut. It's never too early to learn this lesson about creativity and Vonnegut was teaching it to high school kids.

In 2006, the year before he died, a group of students at Xavier High School in New York, wrote to their favourite authors as part of an assignment, asking them to come and visit their school.

Vonnegut was the only one to respond, and while he said he would not be able to make it in person, he did send the following letter.

Dear Xavier High School, and Ms. Lockwood, and Messrs Perin, McFeely, Batten, Maurer and Congiusta:

I thank you for your friendly letters. You sure know how to cheer up a really old geezer (84) in his sunset years. I don't make public appearances any more because I now resemble nothing so much as an iguana.

What I had to say to you, moreover, would not take long, to wit: Practice any art, music, singing, dancing, acting, drawing, painting, sculpting, poetry, fiction, essays, reportage, no matter how well or badly, not to get money and fame, but to experience becoming, to find out what's inside you, to make your soul grow.

Seriously! I mean starting right now, do art and do it for the rest of your lives. Draw a funny or nice picture of Ms. Lockwood, and give it to her. Dance home after school, and sing in the shower and on and on. Make a face in your mashed potatoes. Pretend you're Count Dracula.

Here's an assignment for tonight, and I hope Ms. Lockwood will flunk you if you don't do it: Write a six line poem, about anything, but rhymed. No fair tennis without a net. Make it as good as you possibly can. But don't tell anybody what you're doing. Don't show it or recite it to anybody, not even your girlfriend or parents or whatever, or Ms. Lockwood. OK?

Tear it up into teeny-weeny pieces, and discard them into widely separated trash recepticals [sic]. You will find that you have already been gloriously rewarded for your poem. You have experienced becoming, learned a lot more about what's inside you, and you have made your soul grow.

God bless you all!

Kurt Vonnegut
Reproduced with permission of Xavier High School

DECISION MAKING

FIGURE OUT THE REAL ISSUE AND STOP FAFFING

'I wish it need not have happened in my time', said Frodo. 'So do I', said Gandalf, 'and so do all who live to see such times. But that is not for them to decide. All we have to decide is what to do with the time that is given us'.

– from *The Fellowship of the Ring* by J.R.R. Tolkien

D ecision making can be tough. I know someone who recently got two amazing job offers – one to move to another company, the other counter offer to stay put. They agonized over it for weeks and even now, having made the decision, they're still not sure whether they made the right one.

In the past, I too have been guilty of spending endless hours of my life faffing over decisions. Looking back, I really wish I'd had a few ground rules – some basic frame of reference that might have helped me. That's what this chapter is about.

It's a four-step method for decision making.

Here's what to do:

1. State the issue.
2. Say what the ideal solution would be.
3. Identify a range of solutions.
4. Pick one.

Here they are in turn.

1 State the issue

Insofar as you can, try to figure out what the real issue is. Be aware that sometimes:

- The stated issue is not the real issue. For example, somebody might have suggested that the issue is that 'revenues are down'. But in fact, the problem could be a bad product or service that customers aren't interested in buying.

- An issue is described by stating a solution to the issue – 'We need to increase revenues' – whereas maybe the problem might be 'we need to sort out the sales department'.
- Even if the issue is stated correctly, there may be a bigger issue and you need to pull back and consider that. 'Revenues are down' but the problem is that our competitors have developed a product that we currently don't have the capability to match.

A particularly good technique of nailing what the real issue is to solve is called 'The 5 Whys'. This is where you state what you believe to be the issue but then ask the question 'Why?' You do this repeatedly. So, for example, 'The issue is that revenues are down'. Why? 'We're not getting enough leads'. Why? 'We're not doing enough cold-calling'. Why? 'Nobody likes to do it and we don't think it's that productive anyway'. So maybe the actual issue is to find other ways of generating leads, for example, through partnering with other companies, referral programmes etc.

2 Say what the ideal solution would be

If you could wave a magic wand, what would be the best possible outcome?

3 Identify a range of solutions

Make a list of all the possible solutions you can think of. Here are some ideas to help you do this or items that might appear on your list:

- Doing nothing might be an option.
- So too might be to take another reading. See what the issue looks like in a few days. Maybe it's improved/changed.

- Perhaps you need to get more information before you can make a decision.
- Ask other people, 'What would you do in my position?'
- If the issue involves another person, try putting yourself in their shoes.
- Keep saying to yourself that 'there has to be another way'.
- Be creative. Think outside the box. Initially don't reject any idea no matter how whacky or outlandish it might seem.

4 Pick one

Now that you have all these possible solutions, how do you choose? It seems to me that we can picture all of these solutions lying on a spectrum ranging from low risk to high risk. Low risk makes decisions out of fear – 'What will happen if I'm not right?' High risk makes decisions out of a sense of excitement – 'What's the worst that can happen?'

So how do you decide? Well, you could do any of the following:

- First of all ask yourself the two preceding questions – 'What will happen if I'm not right?' and 'What's the worst that can happen?'
- Make a list of the pros and cons.
- Ask yourself how much you'd be prepared to bet on your decision being right.
- Decide to give yourself a present (and what that present will be) if your decision turns out to be right.
- Don't be the one to open hostilities. If the course of action you're considering involves dumping on somebody else, don't take it unless they've already dumped on you.

- Timing is everything. Consider the right moment to carry out your decision – some times may be better than others. For example, I once had a boss that I would never approach with anything on a Monday – he was too grumpy.
- Get the monkey off your back. If a course of action involves you *not* having to do something, that is passing the problem onto someone else, then that clearly has lots of attractions.
- If one course of action doesn't work, try another.
- Don't let things fester.
- If it's potentially harmful, sleep on it.

> *When you're supposed to do something or not supposed to do something, your emotional guidance system lets you know. The trick is to learn to check your ego at the door and start checking your gut instead. Every right decision I've made – every right decision I've ever made – has come from my gut. And every wrong decision I've ever made was a result of me not listening to the greater voice of myself.*
>
> – Oprah Winfrey, American media proprietor, talk show host, Stanford University commencement speech, 15 June 2008[15]

Finally, one of the most profound lessons I learned in my life was about fear. If you are thinking of taking a certain course of action and you are afraid of where it might lead and what the consequences might be, then there is only one way to conquer that fear.

It's to take the course of action.

Feel the fear and do it anyway.

Apart from anything else, it's the title of a great book by Susan Jeffers.[16] If you haven't read it, you should.

Comedian Jim Carrey talks about decision making in his 2014 commencement speech at the Maharishi University of Management.[17] This is part of what he says: '. . . the decisions that we make in this moment, which are based in either love or fear. *So many of us choose our path out of fear disguised as practicality* [my italics]. What we really want seems impossibly out of reach and ridiculous to expect, so we never dare to ask the universe for it'.

EMAIL

STEP AWAY FROM THE COMPUTER!

I like to talk to people. I've got one assistant, one Blackberry. That's my overhead. I don't text that much or email. I like to sit down face-to-face and have a conversation with you. I'm old-fashioned.

– Mark Wahlberg, American actor

Apparently in London, at the very beginning of the twentieth century, many postal districts managed twelve deliveries a day, the first being at 7.15am and the last at 8.30pm. If you think about it, this was almost as good as having email – and this nearly a century before email was invented.

The Victorians have been slated for many things but my sense is that when it came to dealing with the mail, they probably did it well. They probably did it in that solid, sensible, practical way for which they have so often been ridiculed.

I can imagine say, the one o'clock postal delivery coming and the letters being placed on either a small tray, if it was a domestic delivery, or in pigeon holes if it was a business. Then, in due course, the master or mistress of the house or some employee of the business would open the letters and deal with their contents.

The key phrase here is 'in due course'.

The notion that each time a letter arrived someone would immediately tear it open and start dealing with whatever issue it raised would have been laughable to those bewhiskered and crinolined Victorians.

One of the things I do is teach courses in project management. Whenever I teach a course I give it all I've got. For a course that starts at nine, I'll be there at seven and I'll pretty much not leave the room until the course ends at five. I may not eat lunch. I'm in the zone. I teach all my courses using a flipchart – no PowerPoint as a crutch for me. As a result, when the course ends, I'm completely exhausted. I have taught more than 600 of these courses but I'm as tired these days as I was after I taught the very, very first one all those years ago.

When I spend a day teaching a course, I do little else. Something would almost have to be life threatening for me to give it any attention. As a result, the day-to-day business of emails is one of the things that gets put on hold. Recently I taught two two-day project management courses back to back with the result that when I had finally finished, there was a backlog of a couple of hundred emails that needed to be looked at.

I started in on them and had dealt with the lot in just over two hours. I started at the top, of course, with the most recent one and worked my way down. What was particularly satisfying was when one that I had already dealt with meant that several earlier ones were now irrelevant. It was surprising how often this happened. What was also surprising was how I had missed nothing urgent – there was nothing that could not have waited.

I'm not the first person to point out that we have become slaves to email, addicted to it. Nor – do I have to even say it – that most emails are crap? (And that's the ones that aren't spam!)

And it's an easy drug to get hooked on. We wonder what could be waiting for us. In my case, is this the day when an email is going to arrive offering to buy my company or suggesting a film deal on one of my novels? I can't wait to find out. My fingers get itchy. It's all too easy to flip into Outlook and have a look.

Our behaviour with email doesn't just border on the ridiculous. It *is* ridiculous. One of the tools I use in my work is a flipchart marker.

Imagine that every time I saw a flipchart marker I picked it up and started writing with it. You would very quickly be calling the men in the white coats. But this is exactly what we do when our computer goes 'bing!' because an email has arrived.

And the best part of all of is that we feel that we are actually working. A colleague explains how he had 500 emails to clear when he returned from holidays. We sympathize and think what an extraordinarily tough job they have and hard worker they must be. It's a charade.

We feel productive. Yet the couple of hours (or more) a day that we spend on email could easily be replaced by that same couple of hours *once a week*. This whole email thing is a joke. And a bad one.

So, if you're tired of all this; if you've convinced yourself you're working hard when in fact all you're doing is being unproductive; if you're short of time and there never seem to be enough hours in the day, then it's time to kick the email habit. It's time to become the master again, rather than the slave. It's time to take back control.

The following would work perfectly well and we can imagine our Victorian ancestors doing exactly this.

1. Check your email three times a day:
  first when you come into work (removing your top hat and handing it along with your cane and gloves to your secretary);
  then just before you go to lunch (which of course, would probably have been ten or so courses, ending with brandy and a cigar);

and finally, before you go home (to your cluttered house, ador-
    ing wife and perfect children).

2. If something really, truly has to be dealt with – in other words,
    if it's wildly important as we described in the 'Being More Pro-
    ductive' chapter, then do so. Otherwise, leave it.

3. Once a week, starting at the most recent, go through your
    inbox and empty it.

The Victorians. They weren't all bad.

> 'If email had been around before the telephone
> was invented people would have said "hey, forget
> email – with this new telephone invention I can
> actually talk to people"'.
>
> – Anon

FAILURE

IT'S GOOD TO FAIL

Es major andar solo que mal acompañado.

– Spanish proverb which translates as 'Better to travel alone than in bad company'. Can be good advice if certain relationships in your life fail.

n 1985 I worked on a project to develop a laptop computer. Today, a laptop is a piece of consumer electronics but in those days it was revolutionary. Our vision was of executives on the road, arriving at their hotel rooms, downloading their mail, checking the Dow, all the kind of stuff we now take for granted. I led the team which was developing the software.

There came the day when we had to decide what operating system our laptop would run. I wasn't part of the decision-making process – as the project manager, I just needed the decision made. One way or the other. A or B.

The techies assembled to make the decision to choose between two contenders. One was a product called MTOS which the techies quickly explained had it all – multithreaded, multitasking, make your breakfast, lots of other great things – and another, really rather pathetic product called MS-DOS. They spoke of it as though it were dog's poo on the underside of your shoe.

You've guessed it. At this critical fork in the road on our project, we went the wrong way. At about the same time, a rather small company in Seattle called Microsoft was in the process of cutting a deal with a rather large company called IBM for the operating system that IBM would run on its PC.

It would be a few more months before we figured out we had made a mistake. And not just any old mistake. A *monster* mistake. A catastrophic blunder of spectacular proportions. An epic fail. Had we gone the other way, we could have been Compaq. I could have been on my ninth or tenth Ferrari by now.

I've made other mistakes in business which, though not as costly, weren't exactly cheap.

- Not making my company small enough quickly enough when the tech bubble burst. Cost? About $1,000,000.
- A high-risk retail business I invested in recently. Cost? €250,000 approx.
- Buying a house for €420,000 and having to sell it for far less than that.

I won't go on.

And that's just me.

- The captain of the *Titanic* steered his ship into an iceberg because he was going too fast and ignored ice warnings. The cost was over 1,500 people dead (including himself) and an inflation-adjusted loss of $168 million.
- Twice – in 1986 and again in 2003 – NASA lost a Space Shuttle and its crew due to faulty equipment. Cost – 14 dead and an inflation-adjusted financial loss of about $27 billion.
- At the height of the dot.com bubble, AOL bought Time Warner for $182 billion. Nine years later, Time Warner spun off with a market capitalization of $36 billion – a $178 billion loss. The newly separated AOL was valued at only $2.5 billion.
- The First World War started because a small group of very important men made some monumental mistakes and miscalculations. Cost – over 37 million military and civilian deaths.
- And further miscalculations at the end of that war by some other important people, meant that it all restarted 20 years

later, resulting in the biggest single reduction in the world population since the Black Death. Cost – 60 million dead, 2.5% of the world's population.

Enough already.

You learn so much from your mistakes. As one of my uncles, a hugely successful businessman, was fond of quoting, 'The man who never made a mistake never made anything'.

And so it is. I've learned that you should never trust a techie to make a marketing decision. I've learned that when your CEO decides to rebrand the company, it's almost certainly time to fire him. I've learned that I really should have been more careful with money throughout my life. And so on and so on and so on.

I've learned things about myself. I've learned that I'm a risk taker. 'What's the worst that can happen?' will almost be the first words out of my mouth when some new venture appears on the horizon.

My failures have made me a better person. I'm stronger, more resilient, don't get stressed easily, laugh more (and I used to laugh an awful lot anyway). When I started my own company, I didn't just start it with no money, I started it – for reasons I don't have to explain – with a £20,000 debt. The Israeli Air Force has a saying – *'en brera'*. It means 'no alternative' – failure is not an option. And so it was. The failures in my life, the mistakes I had made and consequences that I had ridden out, meant that when this challenge of challenges came, I was ready for it. I believed in myself and reckoned I could do what had to be done. Without that history, I suspect I just would have folded and gone and applied for a job somewhere.

Failures make you smarter. Much of the success of the Normandy landings in 1944 was due to the failure at Dieppe in 1942. Just one illustration of this is before Dieppe, the Allies had assumed that, as part of the invasion of Europe, they would have to assault and capture a deep sea port. This would be required because of the scale of the logistical follow up and support, post-invasion. Dieppe convinced them that there would be huge loss of life in such an assault.

So from this grew the idea of *not* assaulting a port at all but rather *creating* one. This was the genesis of the so-called Mulberry artificial harbours and PLUTO (pipeline under the ocean) which supplied fuel to the allied army.

Failures make life more interesting. Imagine what a dull and small life you would end up leading if you had no failures, if you never risked anything.

Dun & Bradstreet in Malibu[18] has set up a 'Failure Wall' where employees are encouraged to write about their failures. The company feels that it encourages risk taking.

And it has. One example of this risk taking is that the company has now instituted what it calls a 'fast failure model' to get products to market more quickly. Jeff Stibel, the CEO, explains: 'We used to do three- and four-year projects, with dozens of consultants, slowly rolling a product to market. Now, we use the fast-failure model: We have a prototype, put it into beta with customers, and then customers tell us whether we are succeeding or failing.

It's a calculated risk: We learn from incremental failure, and have geometric success'.

It seems to work. The company achieved double-digit growth in 2011, the best in the company's history.

So the next time you have a failure, there are three things to do:

First, come out with your hands up. Take responsibility. Don't blame others or try to find scapegoats. Be upfront. If you blew it, say that you blew it.

Next, learn the lessons. You don't need dozens – just the top two or three – or even just one. 'What's the number one thing I can take away from this debacle?'

And finally, and most important of course, do better next time. When failures deliver lessons, you find that your choices narrow – so that next time you're likely to make a better or much wiser choice.

> *'I have not failed, I've just found ten thousand ways that won't work'.*
> – Thomas Edison

(This is not idle talk on Edison's part. He tested literally thousands of materials when trying to come up with a suitable filament for the incandescent light bulbs we now take for granted.)

And not only will you make a better choice but the choice will be made more easily. Instead of having to weigh pros and cons and agonize over things, the course of action will be much clearer – or even a no-brainer.

You're in good company when you fail. Here's Michael Jordan, the basketball player:

> 'I've missed more than 9,000 shots in my career. I've lost almost 300 games. 26 times I've been trusted to take the game winning shot and missed. I've failed over and over again in my life and that is why I succeed'.

J.K. Rowling believes in failure. This is one of the themes of her (sometimes very funny) 2008 Harvard commencement speech.[19]

'I have asked myself what I wish I had known at my own graduation', she begins. She goes on to speak about 'the benefits of failure' and how 'rock bottom became the solid foundation upon which I rebuilt my life'. (We described that 'rock bottom' earlier in the chapter on *Commitment and Perseverance*.)

So too does Conan O'Brien in his completely hilarious 2000 commencement speech at the same institution.[20] He describes graduating, then working for a year on a small cable TV show before being fired. After that he took a series of dead end jobs before getting back into TV. His new show was canned after four weeks.

Then finally he got his big break on *Saturday Night Live*. He was hugely successful and so, on the crest of this wave, he left the show after two seasons to write a TV sitcom. It bombed. But then he moved onto *The Simpsons* and then *Late Night* and found success again.

His life is a rollercoaster of alternating success and failure and this is what he says:

> *'And each time it was bruising and tumultuous. And yet, every failure was freeing, and today I'm as nostalgic for the bad as I am for the good.*
>
> *So, that's what I wish for all of you: the bad as well as the good. Fall down, make a mess, break something occasionally. And remember that the story is never over'.*

And finally here's one for your wall from Nobel Prize winner Samuel Beckett. (It's almost certainly the only writing of his that I've ever read.)

> *'Ever tried. Ever failed. No matter. Try Again. Fail again. Fail better'.*

HAVING A PURPOSE

FIND SOMETHING YOU LIKE TO DO AND YOU'LL NEVER WORK A DAY IN YOUR LIFE

True glory consists in doing what deserves to be written, in writing what deserves to be read, and in so living as to make the world happier and better for our living in it.

— Pliny the Elder, Roman author and philosopher

I f you don't have a purpose in life, what's the point in being alive? I'm with Marie Forleo (www.marieforleo.com) on this one – the world *does* need that special gift *that only you have.*

If you're lucky, you (a) discover your passion and (b) it becomes how you earn your crust. This is what has happened to my son, Hugh. He's a political journalist and loves what he does.

Do this now. Find on YouTube a piece of video of Sir Richard Branson and watch it for 30 seconds. He's clearly having a ball – he loves what he does. Read bestselling author, Manda Scott's biography on her website http://www.mandascott.co.uk/ – the piece that begins 'Writing is the best job in the world'. Watch a video of your favourite band. These people love what they do.

Find your passion and spend time on it and you'll bounce out of bed in the morning eager to face the day. Those days will fly by happily. You may tumble into bed at night dog tired because of the hours you've put in, but it won't have seemed like work at all. The difference between weekdays and weekends will blur. You'll feel a joy and a satisfaction that you could never have even remotely imagined clocking in or working for the man.

> *Your time is limited, so don't waste it living someone else's life. Don't be trapped by dogma – which is living with the results of other people's thinking. Don't let the noise of others' opinions drown out your own inner voice. And most important, have the courage to follow your heart and intuition. They somehow already know what you truly want to become. Everything else is secondary.*
>
> Steve Jobs, American entrepreneur, Stanford University commencement speech, 2005[21]

I don't earn all my crust from my books but I absolutely can't complain. I've discovered my passion – writing fiction – and I'm spending more and more time at it and making increasing amounts of money from it every year.

So there are two things you've got to do. They are:

- Find your passion.
- See if you can make a living from it. Failing that see if you can spend more and more time at it.

This, more than anything else, is the thing I wish I'd know when I started working.

Find your passion

Here are two ways to do that.

First, figure out and write down how you'd like to spend your days. Don't put any limitations on yourself here. It's really the what-if-I-won-the-lottery question. Yes, sure you might take some holidays and buy lots of 'stuff' and eat and drink in the best places but sooner or later you'd get tired of that and then you'd have to decide what you're going to do with your time. What is it you'd really love to do every day if you could?

Secondly – and this is the best and perhaps the only real way to find your passion – simply go and try things and see what you like best.

> *'Clarity comes from engagement, not thought'.*
> – Marie Forleo, American author[22]

I'm a perfect example of this. I love music. All kinds of music. I've even come to like country music (if you're interested, it was a song by The Notorious Cherry Bombs[23] that converted me). And so ever since I was a teenager I've thought I'd love to play music; I thought music might be my passion.

Over the years I've tried drums, the guitar and the piano. But each time I found that I felt no passion to *play*. I didn't rush home from school thinking of nothing else but wanting to sit at my drum kit and practice. I didn't look forward eagerly to the next piano lesson, practising for hours on end so as to impress my teacher. I realized that while I might have had a passion for listening to or discovering music, I really had no passion to play it. If I am going to be a concert pianist it's not going to be in this life.

But ask me to write a story – to start creating a setting and imaginary friends and situations and I'm off. In parallel with writing this book, I've just begun to get a new novel off the ground. It's my passion and I could hardly be happier. And if I did win the lottery I probably wouldn't be spending my time much differently from the way I do at the moment.

So no problem if you're not really sure what your passion is. You'll have a hunch – some possibilities. So just try something. Engage with it. Give it a shot. You'll find out quickly enough if it excites you or not. If it does, you're in business. If not, then that's no problem. Just move on and try something else.

You can try lots of things. And you would find this book – *The First 20 Hours: How to Learn Anything Fast*[24] – a great help. It would mean you could power through lots of things until you find the one that you like best.

Great book this. It may indeed be true that in order to master something you have to spend the supposed 10,000 hours on it, but this book shows you that you can acquire a working knowledge of something in as little as 20 hours. A completely how-to book as the author tests his theory on skills as diverse as yoga, playing the ukulele, programming a web application, touch typing, windsurfing and playing 'Go', one of the world's oldest board games.

See if you can make a living from it

> *'Most men lead lives of quiet desperation and go to the grave with the song still in them'.*
>
> – Henry David Thoreau, American author, poet and philosopher

Life isn't a rehearsal. You get one shot at it. It's going to be an unhappy life indeed if you're not living your passion. But the mortgage has to be paid, the family fed and you want to be happy.

So can you find a way to make money from your passion? With the internet it's more possible than ever. The most unlikely things have become businesses on the internet. If you're in any doubt about that statement, check out the website, 'America's Weirdest Businesses'.[25]

And if you want to see how somebody looks and behaves and feels when they're pursuing their passion and making money from it, check out http://www.marieforleo.com/. Like her or loathe her, when's the last time you were that buzzed up about what you do?

Almost certainly there are other people who share your passion. Is there something you can make or do or sell that they will pay for? As I said at the beginning, if you're lucky you'll find you can make a living from it – or even become rich. Plenty of people have done that.

Here's a person who made a living from what they loved. Richard Gough is former Scotland international and Rangers captain. This is what he said. 'I was fortunate to play football for my living which was a childhood dream. So in all honesty I would not have changed much'.

(As an aside, he added, 'One thing I would have changed was to not be as stubborn as I was in certain situations and definitely to have been more politically correct. But to be fair, that was not my personality so I don't really know how that would have worked!!')

But even if that's not what happens and you don't get to earn your living from your passion, it's not a problem. You can get yourself a BJ![26] 'BJ' stands for 'bridge job' – something you do to pay the bills while you pursue your passion.

I started ETP, my company, not to be rich but so that I could spend more time on my passion. It's worked. ETP is my BJ (and has been since 1992) while I continue to write fiction. And happily my bridge job is something I like doing too. And indeed since writing is a very solitary occupation, it's probably good that I am out in the real world meeting lots of real people which is what my bridge job causes me to do.

Spend your time working on whatever you are passionate about in life. If your degree was focused upon one particular area, don't let that stop you moving in another direction. If college hasn't worked out for you, don't let that put you off. . . . You may decide to take a break and consider your options. I would urge you to travel, take on new experiences and draw upon those when it comes to making the decisions that will shape your future. The amount of business ideas that people pick up from travelling the world is enormous.

– Sir Richard Branson, British entrepreneur, commencement speech, Class of 2013, LinkedIn, 21 May 2013[27]

KEEPING YOUR BUSINESS GOING

DON'T RUN OUT OF MONEY

Number one, cash is king.

— Jack Welch, American business executive

You may decide that, arising out of your passion (the previous chapter), you're going to start your own business. Good for you.

If you do, then hopefully you're not starting your own business just to make money. Sure, money is important and making lots of it would be a very nice thing indeed. But I'd like to think your primary reason for starting your own thing is that you're passionate about it.

But in one sense, running your own business *is* all about the money. Once you get your business up and running – by which I mean from the moment the gun goes off and you're out there hawking your wares, there's one consideration that overrides all others. In a sense it's the only rule of running your own business.

Don't run out of money.

Here are the things I have learned in this regard. Most of them are stating the bleeding obvious. Despite this, most of them have all been learned by me at some cost, financial and otherwise.

Your customers better have money

Whatever business you decide to go into, make sure that whatever customers you start to court have money. There's nothing worse (or more useless) that customers who *don't* have money. The retail business I invested in – even though it bombed – was correct in this sense. It targeted people who had money.

Premium pricing or be expensive

Here's something I learned at no cost and it has served me well down the years. Although it wouldn't be applicable to all industries. For example, if you're setting out to be the cut price darling of your sector, it doesn't apply. But I'll tell you what it is anyway and you can draw your own conclusions.

Unless you've been living on Mars for the last 15 years, you've heard of Ryanair. It's named after its founder, the late Tony Ryan. But Tony Ryan also started another enterprise called GPA, at one point the world's largest commercial aircraft leasing company.

The story goes that just before Ryan started GPA, when he was still an employee of Aer Lingus, he was in Thailand on company business. He was thinking of starting his own thing and wondering what sort of business he should get into. He happened to look out the window of his hotel room and saw a street vendor selling snacks for a few baht. Ryan thought about how many snacks the guy would have to sell to make any kind of a living. And so, the story goes, Ryan resolved that he would go into an expensive business. Hence, aircraft leasing.

I took this lesson on board when I started my business. I had no experience of selling so assumed I wouldn't be very good at it and therefore wouldn't make many sales. Thus, my thinking went, any sale I did make better count – and count big. So we started out expensive – and have been ever since. Even when prices of certain of our offerings have eroded we have stayed very much on the high side. (We reckon that if we lose about 10% of business because of price, we have it about right.)

An interesting angle on this is the following: for years I have had a sales conversion rate of almost exactly 50%. In other words, half the proposals I send out result in business, the other half go away for a variety of reasons – things change at the customer's, we're too expensive, the person I was dealing with leaves and so on. Recently I stopped offering some of the standard discounts we offer on our pricing which meant that our pricing effectively increased.

Result?

My sales conversion rate went *up* to 75%.

Go figure.

Bad debts and getting stung

We're lucky to operate in a sector where bad debts are rare. As far as I can remember we've only had one in our career and that was when I spoke at a conference and then found out that the organizers had gone bust. Boy, did we learn from that. Now we get paid upfront.

So make sure you don't put yourself in a position where you're going to get stung. Ask yourself what happens if they cancel? Or if they go bust? It's risk management – what are the things that could happen that could cause you not to get your money? And what can you do to stop these things from happening? Or how do you deal with them if they do?

And when you do get stung, as you almost certainly will, learn from it. Learn big and learn quickly. As the saying goes, 'Fool me once, shame on you. Fool me twice, shame on me'.

The job's not over until the money's in the bank

I have a colleague, Karen, who manages our company's finances. The woman should be Minister for Finance or Chancellor of the Exchequer. If there's a (financially) more well-managed company than ours on the planet, I'd like to know about it.

One of Karen's many great ideas was the 5% early payment discount, which she dreamt up 10 or 12 years ago. A simple idea. Pay early and you get a 5% discount. I've literally lost count of the number of times this has saved our bacon – especially in the last few years of economic depression.

Remember that the job's not over until the money's in the bank and Karen's 5% early payment discount has been/is one way of ensuring exactly that.

If you get into trouble

I don't know of any business that hasn't had periods of financial trouble over the years. Ours is no exception. But whenever those periods have come along, we've found that it's possible to do deals with everyone – even the taxman.

Ultimately, it's simple. Everybody wants to get their money. And while, in certain circumstances, it's possible to walk away from debts, I've never been a great believer in that. Legally it may be possible. Financially it may be a no-brainer. But karmically you're on thin ice, I think. So I've never done it. If that makes me the biggest fool on the planet, so be it.

So if you get into trouble, be straight with your creditors. Tell them your situation, that you want them to get their money but that they're going to have to do a deal. Most creditors will know that situation only too well. In all likelihood, they'll have been in exactly that place themselves sometime.

We all support each other and everybody wins.

> *'There is only one boss. The customer. And he can fire everybody in the company from the chairman on down, simply by taking his money somewhere else'.*
>
> – Sam Walton, founder of Wal-Mart

MAKING THE SALE

PEOPLE DON'T LIKE TO BE SOLD TO – BUT THEY LOVE TO BUY

Everyone lives by selling something.

– Robert Louis Stevenson, Scottish writer and poet

I f you do start your own business, apart from not running out of money, the only other thing that matters is sales. You're going to have to make them. Lots of them. Over and over again.

When I started my own business in 1992, I had never done any selling. Well actually, that's not entirely true. I had had some jobs prior to that, so clearly I had sold myself to some employers.

And so in fact, if you think you've got no selling experience, then this may not be entirely true. If you've ever had any kind of job, temporary, permanent, whatever – then you already have some selling experience and, I think you'll agree, that's a start.

When I started my own thing, sales was the thing that concerned me most. Actually, 'concerned' would be the understatement of the year. I was *terrified* at the prospect of having to go out and sell; terrified that my livelihood would depend on my ability to do this.

And whether you're terrified of sales or not, sales should concern you. If you run your own business, then without sales there is no business. And if you work for an organization, you're still going to have to sell – sell your ideas, sell your proposals and plans, sell yourself, if you go looking for a pay rise or a promotion, for example.

These are the things I wish I'd known about selling.

People don't buy what you sell, they buy what you believe

I'm astonished that more people haven't cottoned on to this. I have to stress too that I didn't figure it out – until I came across this Simon Sinek TED talk.[28] Let me give you the gist of his message.

I'm astonished that companies spend billions of dollars on advertising every year and that the vast bulk of that money is completely down the drain. I'm astonished that clearly highly paid and highly intelligent people haven't either figured this out or that somebody hasn't told them.

Recently I heard a radio ad for a certain brand of car. The ad went on to say that this car was the fastest growing car brand in Ireland. Yawn! Who cares? But, if you think about it, the vast majority of ads are like this – they talk about certain aspects of the product or service being sold – it's got better technology or features, the prices are down, it's new and so on and so on.

But who cares about most of this stuff? What people care about . . . the thing that gets people passionate . . . excited . . . eager to buy . . . reaching for their purse or wallet or credit card . . . is none of these things. It's not the spec sheet of the product or service you're selling. The thing that gets them eager to buy is why you're in business. Why are you passionate about what you do and why does that make a difference?

Ryanair – like them or loathe them – they're passionate about safe, cheap air travel. Tiffany, the jewellers – they're passionate about romance. You can buy rings from millions of places. You can only buy a Tiffany ring in one place. Apple – they're passionate about building great products that challenge the status quo. This is the heart of Sinek's message.

As I mentioned, I started my business, ETP (www.etpint.com) in 1992. ETP is a project management training and consulting company. Project management was and still is a field that is *crammed* with competitors – everybody from the big consulting companies to the guy who buys a book and suddenly starts offering training. Every competitor I've ever come across sells project management as rocket science – it's complicated, sometimes incredibly so.

My hunch was that it wasn't complicated at all – that it was just common sense. And so that was what I believed – then and now. And that was what I started to sell. This gave me my USP – Unique Selling Proposition. Everything flowed from that.

People don't buy what you do – they buy why you do it. They buy your passion for your offering.

Figure that out and your selling will be pretty straightforward.

> *'Obstacles are necessary for success because in selling, as in all careers of importance, victory comes only after many struggles and countless defeats'.*
>
> – Og Mandino, author of *The Greatest Salesman in the World*[29]

Love your customers

There's an old gag that goes, 'The secret to successful selling is sincerity. If you can fake that, you'll be really great at it'. Like all good gags, it has a germ of truth in it. The secret to successful selling *is* sincerity. Not faked but real.

You have to love your customers.

I don't mean this in some kind of abstract way – in the way, for example, that all companies say they love their customers. Neither do I mean it as I love them because their money pays *my* bills and gives me *my* income. I mean it that *I love* my customers. I love them as though they were my friends, relatives, loved ones.

When I come across a potential new customer, I love them. I want to help them. I want to make their lives better and happier – and I know that what I sell can do that. It hurts me to see them suffering because of badly run projects, the associated late nights and weekends and what all of that does to their lives. If this potential customer were my wife or child, I wouldn't want them to suffer like that for a moment longer.

That is how I love them.

Recently I had a bad experience with a particular travel booking website. On those rare occasions – and they have been rare – when somebody has had a bad experience with our company, we have not just increased the love – we have love bombed them.

By comparison, I've heard nothing back from them. They don't love me. And as a result, I will not be buying anything from them again.

You gotta have daily targets

I remember days – when we were starting out – where we had no customers, no money due to come in, no sales in the pipeline, personal and company debts piling up. It's hard to drag yourself out of bed in those situations.

These days, I still do cold calling. Anyone who's ever done it will tell you that it's not the most life-enhancing thing you can do. But it has to be done. That pesky tree has to be shaken.

And, as we said already, sales are the lifeblood of your company. You can never stop.

And so, you have to have targets.

I'm going to make so many calls today. I'm going to make one more today than I made yesterday. I'm going to try to achieve one (or two or ten or a thousand or whatever it is) sales every day. I have to hit this target this month. To do that I have to do so many sales every week and that translates into so much sales activity I have to do today. Targets. Targets. Targets.

The day is where you'll win it or lose it. Do the sales activity – make the calls, send the emails, have the meetings – every day and you'll be fine.

So, in conclusion: be passionate about what you're selling. Love the people you sell to – make their lives better by what you give them. And have targets – especially for those times when the going gets tough.

MANAGING PEOPLE

HOW OUR NATURAL TENDENCY TO MANAGE IS OFTEN THE OPPOSITE OF WHAT WE OUGHT TO DO

Most of what we call management consists of making it difficult for people to get their work done.

— Peter Drucker, American management writer and theorist

n 1980 I got sent on a project management course. It was a residential course in a really nice seaside hotel in the south of England. I can't remember if the course was a week or two weeks long. Anyway, however long it was, it felt much longer! We worked days, evenings and nights on a really stupid case study from which we learned (and I remember) absolutely nothing. (In fairness, I should also add that while the course was rubbish, the food in the hotel was really rather good.)

On the last afternoon of the last day – a Friday – we were there in the room, bags packed, ready to catch trains and planes, when one of the two instructors started to talk about managing people. What he said in the next hour gave me one of the biggest light bulb moments of my career.

What follows here is the gist of what he said along with some of my own experience grafted on to it. There are really only two points I want to make.

One size doesn't fit everybody

It's true to say that each of us, depending on our personality, has what could be called our 'natural' management style. Some people are very hands off. 'There's no point in having a dog', the saying goes, 'and barking yourself'. In other words, if somebody has a job to do let them get on with it and trust that they will do it properly. Then, on the other end of the spectrum, there are people who are very hands-on. Only by micromanaging everything do they feel that they're in control and can be sure that things are on track. Control freaks.

Which is right? The former sounds like a nice regime to work under – the person being managed can use their own initiative and creativity – but it sounds like things could go a long way wrong here before they were spotted. The latter regime sounds a lot more safe and secure, but it also sounds like it could be a giant pain to work under (or indeed to have to apply) such a regime.

The answer, of course, is that one size doesn't fit everybody and that no matter what your personality causes you to do 'naturally', you're going to have to be a bit more versatile when it comes to managing people.

- Where the evidence is that when you give them a job, it gets done, then leave them alone and let them get on with it. This is true even if your natural style is to micromanage. This will only be counterproductive here. 'If it ain't broke don't fix it' – and it isn't broke here. And the key, of course, is evidence. The facts. This isn't about whether you like somebody or think they're smelly or would loan them 20 quid. It's all based on facts. When you give them a job, it gets done. Or not.
- Where:
  - somebody doesn't report to you – somebody in another group or department or organization; or
  - is inexperienced; or
  - you're unsure about their ability;

  then you need to stay on their case a bit (or a lot) more. This is where micromanagement is good and hands-off would be very bad – again, irrespective of what your personality drives you to do.

'People often say that motivation doesn't last. Well, neither does bathing – that's why we recommend it daily'.

– Zig Ziglar, American author and motivational speaker

What we ought to do versus our natural tendency

Good management means we spend our management time where it will make the most difference. If it ain't broke, don't fix it is one end of the spectrum; the other is where things are very broke and where most of the foul-ups and firefighting will occur. So we should spend most of our time on the 'broke' end of the spectrum.

I think for most people, including myself, our natural tendency is to do the opposite of that. Here's why.

What do we want from work? Yes, we want to earn some money, we want it to be interesting, we'd like to be with nice people but, in a nutshell, we want to have some fun. We're going to spend a large proportion of our life in work. It can't be a vale of tears all the time. And the 'ain't broke' end of the spectrum is fun. You spend the week at this end of the spectrum and when you go home on Friday you'll be whistling. You'll be saying, 'I made a great decision coming to work here. Interesting work. Great people. I can't believe it's Friday already. I wish it wasn't the weekend'. (Well okay – maybe not quite that!)

Now imagine you spend a week at the broke end of the spectrum. You'll go home and you'll kick the cat. Because over here is foul-ups, screw-ups, difficult conversations, getting your ass chewed off, embarrassment, having to eat humble pie and so on. We want this like we want a hole in the head.

And so, as human beings who just want to be happy, we have a tendency to gravitate towards the 'ain't broke' end of the spectrum. We'd much rather hang out with the good guys.

Even though I'm aware of it, I have this tendency myself to this day. Here's how it works for me.

On Monday I'll sort out any problem for you. I'm firmly at the broke end of the spectrum.

By Wednesday I'm drifting a bit. There'll be some problem or issue and I'll find myself saying things like, 'Ah, maybe it's not as serious as all that' or 'I might just leave it a few more days and see if it sorts itself out'.

And by Friday afternoon, I'm firmly in 'girls just want to have fun' mode. Don't ask me to deal with difficult issues on Friday afternoon because I won't be a happy bunny.

And I suspect I'm not alone in this.

Don't get me wrong. I'm not saying we shouldn't have a bit of fun at work. I'm not saying we shouldn't socialize or hang out with the good guys.

But be clear what you're doing. You're socializing. You're hanging out. On the 'ain't broke' end of the spectrum, they don't need management – or at least not much of it. Over on the other end of the spectrum is where most of your management time needs to go and be spent.

This is the key thing I learned about managing people – that our natural tendency is almost the exact opposite of what we should be doing. It was a profound eye-opener and a lifelong lesson for me.

MEETINGS

JUST BECAUSE EVERYONE
ELSE GOES DOESN'T
MEAN YOU HAVE TO

*If you had to identify, in one word, the reason why the
human race has not achieved, and never will achieve,
its full potential, that word would be 'meetings'.*

– Dave Barry, American author and columnist

P lease may I say this with all of the passion that I can possibly summon up?

Most meetings are a complete waste of time.

May I say furthermore, that the person who invented that feature in Outlook where you can book other people's time for your meeting, should be clapped in irons and sent to Devil's Island with no possibility of sentence remission – given that he or she has wiped out more of people's lives than many small wars.

Please don't misunderstand or misquote me on this. I'm not saying that all meetings are crap. Some meetings are incredibly important and useful. But I would have to say that if I looked back over my career and thought of the amount of time I have spent at meetings, I believe I would have to say that at least 75% of it was completely wasted. And further, if I could have that time back – which I can't, of course – I'd be a very competent jazz pianist. (If that was my passion – which it isn't, as you know. But that's a different chapter!) I don't do regrets – I think they're pretty pointless. But if I did, this would surely have to be one of them.

You don't want to end up with the same regret.

So first are a few simple rules for holding effective meetings. I've used them for years and they work. The rules are designed to help you run your meetings properly and to get others to do the same.

Every organization has a culture and part of that culture is how its meetings are run. But just because they've been run a certain way in the past doesn't mean they have to be run like that going forward. Be clear – it's okay for you to step up, take action and propose these simple rules.

Holding effective meetings

1. Do we really need to meet? If you're going to take some of other people's precious time away from them, you'd better have a damn good reason!

2. Who *really* needs to be at this meeting? Once again – if you are going to take some of other people's precious time away from them, you'd better have a damn good reason! So is this person going to provide useful input to this meeting? Are they essential to getting the result you want?

3. A meeting is a little mini-project. Therefore it needs:
   a goal (what's the meeting trying to accomplish?);
   a plan (an agenda, i.e. what we are going to do at the meeting which will result in the achievement of the goal?);
   a leader (chairperson).

4. Decline/refuse/don't go if you're not given these three things.

5. Be on time.

6. No multitasking – no device usage unless necessary for meeting.

7. If you're not getting anything out of the meeting, it should be okay to leave.

8. Meetings are not for information sharing – that should be done before the meeting via email and/or the agenda. In other words, the meeting isn't the place to read the stuff you should have read before the meeting.

9. Assign action items at the conclusion of the meeting.

10. Don't feel bad about calling people out if they're in breach of any of the above; it's the right thing to do.

If the meeting culture at your organization is out of control and you've tried the simple rules and for whatever reason, you feel they haven't worked, you don't have to become part of the madness; you don't have to join the rest of the lemmings.

And just so you're in no doubt as to what I mean here it's this:

Just because everybody else goes to the meeting doesn't mean that you have to go.

And let's be clear, so nobody's in any doubt, I'm not talking about bunking off. I'm talking about not wasting your precious time at a meeting where your attendance is superfluous.

There are plenty of ways not to go to a meeting:

- You can say, 'Call me if you need me'.
- You can go but say, 'Can I do my bit first?' and then leave.
- You can go. Then place your mobile phone on the table in front of you. After a few minutes, pretend it lit up and pick it up. Look at it with a very serious expression on your face. Say, 'Can you excuse me a minute?' Leave and don't go back.
- Arrange with a colleague to tap on the door and call you out of the meeting.
- If you're the boss you can go to the meeting, get them all started, then leave and come back at the end to hear the result.

And I'm sure there are many others.

As a result of this, one of two things will happen. Either:

- The sky will fall – and then you have your answer. This meeting is important.

- Or else it won't. And now, not only have you saved some of your precious time. But more importantly, you've created a precedent. If you didn't go once you could not go again. And eventually this meeting might just disappear out of your life.

Meetings. Lots of them are crap.

> 'Meetings are indispensable when you don't want to do anything'.
>
> – John Kenneth Galbraith, American economist and diplomat

MOVING UP

SHOW YOU CAN DO WHAT YOU'RE AIMING FOR

You can outwork anybody. Try it, you will find out that you can do it.

– Woody Hayes, head football coach and professor emeritus at The Ohio State University

M

y father was a salesman – apparently, a great one. He used to tell this story.

The Area Sales Manager is going through the office one day and he sees the Salesman in his office. The Salesman isn't making calls or writing proposals or chasing leads or doing any of the stuff that salesmen are meant to be doing. Rather, he has his feet on the desk, is making paper jets and flying them across the office. Apparently he has been doing this for some time – there is a large pile of paper jets on the floor.

The Area Sales Manager comes in and angrily demands to know why the Salesman isn't making calls/writing proposals/chasing leads.

'Go **** yourself', the Salesman says casually.

The Area Sales Manager is outraged. He can hardly believe his ears. Furiously, he storms out of the office, goes to *his* boss, the Regional Sales Manager and tells him what's happened.

The Regional Sales Manager too is very, very angry. He can't have things like this going on in his organization. He accompanies the Area Sales Manager down to the Salesman's office. The pile of paper jets has gotten bigger. The Regional Sales Manager demands to know whether it's true that the Salesman told the Area Sales Manager to go **** himself.

Hardly batting an eyelid, the Salesman says that it is.

'And you can go **** yourself too', he adds.

At this stage both men are incandescent with anger and indignation. As luck would have it, the Head of Sales for the entire company happens to be in the office that day. The Area and Regional Sales Managers go to this exalted person and tell him what's happened. They demand that he take some drastic action with the Salesman.

The Head of Sales accompanies the two men down to the Salesman's office. The Salesman is just putting the finishing touches to another paper jet. The Head of Sales asks the Salesman whether it is true what the two other gentlemen have told him – that he told them to go **** themselves.

'Yes, it's true', the Salesman says agreeably, 'and you can go for a long walk on a short pier'.

Without another word, the Head of Sales turns on his heel and out of the Salesman's office. The two other men scurry after him.

'What are you going to do?' they ask eagerly.

'How's he doing on his targets?' asks the Head of Sales.

Surprised, the two men look at each other.

'I think he's ahead. Isn't he?' the Regional Sales Manager asks the Area Sales Manager.

'Way ahead', admits the Area Sales Manager. 'He's more than 200% over the target'.

The Head of Sales considers this for a moment. Then he starts heading for the front door.

'Where are you going?' the two men ask in surprise.

'I'm going down to the seafront to find a pier', the Head of Sales says. 'You two can make your own arrangements'.

The moral of the story? If you're doing what you said you'd do, then everybody else *can* go **** themselves.

It's the key to getting a raise and the key to getting promoted.

> *If several years ago you stopped challenging yourself, you're going to be bored. If you work for some guy who you used to sit next to, and really, he should be working for you, you're going to feel undervalued, and you won't come back . . . so start thinking about this now, do not leave before you leave. Do not lean back; lean in. Put your foot on that gas pedal and keep it there until the day you have to make a decision, and then make a decision . . .*
>
> *What about the rat race in the first place? Is it worthwhile? Or are you just buying into someone else's definition of success? Only you can decide that, and you'll have to decide it over and over and over. But if you think it's a rat race, before you drop out, take a deep breath. Maybe you picked the wrong job. Try again. And then try again. Try until you find something that stirs your passion, a job that matters to you and matters to others. It is the ultimate luxury to combine passion and contribution. It's also a very clear path to happiness.*
>
> Sheryl Sandberg, American technology executive, activist, and author, Barnard College commencement speech, 17 May 2011[30]

Getting a raise

I know somebody who recently got a 40% salary hike! In the current economic climate!! In doing so they turned down what would have been a 50% salary hike to go to a competitor.

Here's how he did it:

1. He *proved* he was doing an outstanding job. Just like the Salesman in my story, his job had measures and he showed that he was exceeding them. Significantly. If your job has measures then proving that you're exceeding them is idiotically simple. If your job doesn't have measures, then it's impossible.

2. If your job doesn't have measures you need to go and work with your boss to put some in place. It's the conversation that begins with the words, 'Hey boss, when the end of the year comes, how would we both know that I've done an amazing job?' Don't bring your boss problems, bring solutions – propose some measures. Without measures, it's impossible to know if you're doing a good job or not. And then it becomes very difficult to ask for anything other than a fairly paltry raise. And you might still get stiff resistance to that.

3. Back to my story. That person got another offer. You don't have to do this but it certainly focuses the boss's mind. Provided you have measures and provided you are exceeding them, then the decision to pay you more is going to become something of a no-brainer.

4. He asked for a raise. Whether you have another offer or not, with you exceeding your measures, it's hard to see how they could turn you down. Again, don't bring them problems, bring them solutions. Explain the salary you'd like and how your performance against *that* would get measured. You're already teeing up your *next* raise.

Getting promoted

To get promoted, to move up or get ahead, you need to show that you can do the job you're aiming for. The simplest way to do this is with the idea of 'acting as if'.

'Acting as if' is a simple idea. The way you do it is that you try to behave – as far as possible – as though you already had the new job.

> 'Whenever you are asked if you can do a job, tell 'em "Certainly, I can!" Then get busy and find out how to do it'.
>
> **– Theodore Roosevelt, 26th President of the United States**

Here are some ways of doing that.

- Ask yourself, if you had this new job, what are the measures of success, i.e. how would you know if you had been outstandingly successful? Do you have all the necessary skills and/or qualifications to achieve these measures? If not, what are you going to do about that? Are there certain tools that you need to do that new job? If so, maybe you need to be getting your hands on these and familiarizing yourself with them.
- Imagine what a typical day in this new job would be like? Picture the challenges you would be faced with. How would you deal with those challenges? What people would you have to deal

with? Would you be up to coping with those people? What do you even know about those people? How can you find out more? How can you make your current day more like that typical day?

- Are there things you do now which you wouldn't have to do in the job you're going after? If so, can you find ways of getting rid of them? And similarly, are there aspects of the job you're going after that you could start to do now? Could you offer to take on some extra responsibilities (and maybe shed some to counterbalance that)?

- When you go to meetings or presentations, attend them as though you already had this new job. What kind of things would you be hoping to achieve from these meetings or get from these presentations? What points would you be making? Presumably you would view these things from a different standpoint from where you are at the moment. What would that standpoint be?

- Imagine you had the new salary package that goes with this new job. What would that be like? Are there things you'd be able to do that you can't do now?

- Are there things that you worry about now that you wouldn't have to worry about in the job you're going after? If so, could you stop fretting about them now? And equally, what are the things that you'll have to concern yourself with if you get this new job? How do you feel about those? Will there be a lot more stress involved? Do you want that stress? Will you be able to cope with it?

- Are you ready for the transition to your new job when it comes? If you had to do it right now – I mean, if at this instant, you were told you had the job, what things would you have to get sorted before you could take it up?

All of these things are candidates for being done now.

By acting as if, when the time comes to compete for this job, you'll be in pole position. On the application form, at the interview, you'll be able to talk authoritatively of what the world would be like if you got this job.

Do that and you're most of the way there.

You have a choice. You can either be a passive victim of circumstance or you can be the active hero of your own life. Action is the antidote to apathy and cynicism and despair. You will inevitably make mistakes. Learn what you can and move on. At the end of your days, you will be judged by your gallop, not by your stumble.

– Bradley Whitford, American actor, University of Wisconsin-Madison commencement speech, 15 May 2004[31]

NEGOTIATION

THERE MUST BE SOMETHING IN THE DEAL FOR EVERYONE

My father said: 'You must never try to make all the money that's in a deal. Let the other fellow make some money too, because if you have a reputation for always making all the money, you won't have many deals'.

– J. Paul Getty, American industrialist and billionaire

I f you've ever flown across the Atlantic you'll most likely have seen ads in the in-flight magazine for negotiating seminars. The tagline is a good one. 'In Business as in Life', they blare, 'You Don't Get What You Deserve. You Get What You Negotiate'.

Maybe it's true. I've never done one of these seminars. So anything I've learned about negotiation I've picked up along the way. There have been a couple of negotiations, in particular, that I really fouled up very badly. And it would be true to say that had I done them differently, my life might well have taken a different (or maybe a very different) course.

What I now realize is that the basic principle is win–win. There has to be something in the negotiation ('the deal') for everybody. Of course, Stephen Covey pointed this out a long time ago in his wonderful, *The 7 Habits of Highly Effective People*.[32] Habit 4 is to 'Think Win/Win'.

With this in mind, these are some of the things that I now know.

Think win/win

These days when I negotiate and do a deal with somebody, I try to see it both from my point of view and from their's. If they're not getting some or all of what they want from the deal, then I may as well forget it. It's not going to work. Even if we manage to reach a deal, if there isn't a sufficiently good win in there for them, then there's a good chance that the deal will unravel or fall apart in its implementation.

A win/win deal should work like a well-oiled machine. Everybody's getting something from it. Why would anyone in their right mind want to welsh on a deal like that?

50/50 is good

A few years after I started in business, I put together a partnership deal with somebody else. I had worked with them before. We got on well. But the deal was very baroque/complicated. For different levels of performance, they received different levels of reward. After it got rolling, the deal also went through a couple of revisions. (This often happens when the theoretical deal actually starts to get implemented in practice. Things become clearer, assumptions turn out not to be true, it doesn't quite operate in the way that was expected.)

These revisions made the deal even more complicated. What was worse, we now had two different interpretations of what had been agreed. To cut a long story short, the deal fell apart.

So these days, if I'm looking at a deal, I start from the point of view of 50/50. In the spirit of win/win, if both sides are doing equal amounts of work, both sides should share equally. I think of win/win as one end of a spectrum.

The other end is what I think of as a finder's fee. If they are doing almost no work and I am doing most of the work, but I still get benefit from the deal then maybe a 10% (or so) finder's fee is more appropriate.

The rewards from the deal should be proportional to the amount of work each side has to put in. There *is* no such thing as a free lunch. Don't go looking for one.

And equally, an age-old piece of advice, 'If a deal sounds too good to be true, then it probably is'. Keep that in mind and it should keep you clear of Ponzi schemes that come your way.

Splitting the difference is good

Related to win/win and 50/50 is the idea of splitting the difference. Mostly used to negotiate price it's a way of each side getting some of what they need and – most importantly – the deal not being lost because one or other side digs their heels in.

Giving concessions is good

Giving concessions is a great thing to do in a negotiation. It moves you closer to a deal and it increases the likelihood that things will stay civilized. One of the things I've learned – and this is particularly true when negotiating price – is that if somebody asks for a concession, you should look for one in return.

So, for example, if somebody's looking for a reduction in the price, then sure, you might consider that, but there should be something in return – maybe early payment or they buy more volume or something like that.

Thinking outside the box is good

Sometimes a negotiation bogs down or begins to fall apart because the parties are focused on two entrenched positions. For example, one party is offering x amount of money, the other party is only prepared to accept y.

Well maybe there are other things that can be brought in as part of the negotiation. If the negotiation was centred on money, are there other non-money things, other goods or services, different payment options that could be made part of the negotiation?

We've done this is our training business where rather than reduce the price – and there is huge pressure to do that in recessionary times – we've tried to hold the price but vastly increase what the customer gets for that price.

Backing people into a corner is not good

It may seem like this is a good idea. You back the other side into a corner where you feel they have no other choice but to accept what you're offering.

Don't do it.

This isn't warfare. People *always* have another choice. They can walk away. People *will* cut off their nose to spite their face.

Gloating isn't either

You may land the sweetest deal imaginable and be tempted to crow about it, gloating over how you did it, rubbing it in. You may want to talk about how the other side was in such and such a weak position and as a result of that you were able to pull off this great coup.

Don't do it.

Losers try to get even.

Conflict/arguments are very bad

Walk away. Don't engage. Arguments and conflict rarely do anybody any good.

> 'By fighting you never get enough, but by yielding you get more than you expected'.
>
> – Dale Carnegie, author of How To Win Friends and Influence People[33]

Finally, another way to think about all of this is using the Golden Rule that we met back in the chapter on common sense. Common sense tells you there has to be something in the deal for both parties. Look at it from their point of view. Are they getting most or all of what they want? If they are – and you are too – then it sounds to me like you're in business.

> 'We cannot negotiate with people who say what's mine is mine and what's yours is negotiable'.
>
> – John F. Kennedy, 35th President of the United States

NETWORKING

WHY YOU SHOULD NEVER THROW AWAY A BUSINESS CARD

The mark of a good conversationalist is not that you can talk a lot. The mark is that you can get others to talk a lot. Thus, good schmoozer's are good listeners, not good talkers.

– Guy Kawasaki, American technology evangelist

I got my last 'real' job (i.e. working for somebody else) because somebody I had worked with previously now worked for the company to which I had applied. My first novel was published not because I'd gotten an agent or because I sent lots of submissions to publishers. Rather, it was because the guy who ran a bookshop that I frequented started a publishing company. I met the love of my life because a friend brought a friend to a party that I held.

Bill Gates and Paul Allen, co-founders of Microsoft, met at a computer club meeting about BASIC programming at Seattle's Lakeside School. Steve Jobs and Steve Wozniak met in the early 1970s when Jobs was attending lectures at Hewlett-Packard, where Wozniak worked.

I could go on.

So from today (and I mean *today*), if you haven't already been building your network, you need to start. It will serve you well. It's important if you work for somebody else – and if you decide to start your own thing, it's hard to see how you could survive without it.

So:

Everyone you will ever meet knows something that you don't . . . Respect their knowledge and learn from them. It will bring out the best in all of you.

Bill Nye, Executive Director of The Planetary Society, University of Massachusetts Lowell commencement speech, 17 May 2014[34]

Start collecting business cards

They may be as old as the hills and we may be living in the age of social media but people still use them. Start collecting them. And just as important, have one yourself. If your company doesn't give you one, make one yourself. Or do both. If you can make it memorable that's even better. See, for example, http://mashable .com/2011/07/23/business-card-designs/#.

Start talking to people

In shops, in queues, in waiting rooms, at reception desks, on aeroplanes, buses, trains, just about anywhere there are people – start talking to them. Make small talk. At worst you make a connection. Rarely will you be rebuffed – and if you are, did you really want to have anything to do with that person anyway? Sometimes the small talk will remain just that – small talk. But sometimes small talk can lead to medium-sized talk can lead to big talk and who knows where that could go?

(Especially) if you're in business for yourself, when you're talking to other people who own businesses – no matter how different from yours – ask them how they're doing. 'How's business?' is the easiest opening line in the world. Most people will tell you. It may not be the truth but that doesn't matter. It's an opening.

Then you can find out more. How do they get customers? What things have worked for them and what haven't? How do they think up new things to sell? What's the best idea they ever had? And so on. You may just pick up a gem of an idea.

*Think about
NOT waiting your turn. Instead, think about
getting together with friends that you admire, or envy.
Think about entrepreneuring. Think about NOT waiting for
a company to call you up. Think about not giving your heart
to a bunch of adults you don't know. Think about horizontal
loyalty. Think about turning to people you already know,
who are your friends, or friends of their friends and making
something that makes sense to you together, that is as
beautiful or as true as you can make it.*

– Robert Krulwich, American journalist, Berkeley
Journalism School commencement speech,
7 May 2011[35]

Have an online presence

Get on LinkedIn. It's free and more of the world is arriving every day. Start building your network there. Look for people you've come across and send them invites. Join groups relevant to what you do. Connect to people within those groups.

Set up a Facebook page and/or a website. Get on Twitter. Update regularly. Learn how to use social networking to build your network. I'm no expert on this but there are people who are. They've written books. You can attend courses. There's free stuff on the web.

Start going to events

Get out there and start going to networking events relevant to what you do. There are loads of free ones. There will also be lots that only cost a few euros/pounds/dollars to attend. These could well be even more valuable than the free ones so that the 20/30/40 euros/pounds/dollars it cost you could be money very well spent.

Build a list

Whatever about when you're working for somebody else, this is mandatory if you start your own thing. Try to capture (subject to the usual opt-in requirement) the contact details of:

- Everybody who buys anything from you.
- Anyone who attends anything you speak/perform/appear at.
- Anyone who potentially might buy something from you some time in the future.

Give people who come into your shop/store or onto your website the opportunity to leave their contact details.

Equally make sure all of the preceding groups of people get *your* contact details. Hand out business cards at every available opportunity.

Once you have a list, work it – with newsletters, blogs, special offers and whatever you're having yourself.

And finally – it may help for you to take up golf! I've not done it myself but I probably should have – I'm almost certain I'd have more business as a result. There are certain types of businesses – mine would be one – and certain sectors, for example financial services, where IMHO it will definitely make a difference.

Hang with the
right people. *This is a collaborative world
now. It is a very open collaborative world. You know
that. From Facebook and all the other social media, LinkedIn*
or whatever and hang with the right people because if you
hang with smart people you get smarter and hang with good
people you get gooder.

– Carol Bartz, former Yahoo CEO, University of
Wisconsin-Madison commencement speech,
20 May 2012[36]

ORGANIZATIONS

WHY THEY'RE NOT ACTUALLY RUN BY SENIOR MANAGEMENT

The bottom line is, when people are crystal clear about the most important priorities of the organization and team they work with and prioritized their work around those top priorities, not only are they many times more productive, they discover they have the time they need to have a whole life.

– Stephen Covey, American management theorist and writer

You probably think that your organization is run by the senior management – that that's why they get paid those big salaries and drive those flash cars. Hopefully it's true – and then, there's a sporting chance that you're in good hands.

But in my experience it's much more likely that your organization is being run by Fate/chance/luck. And then there are probably some things you need to be aware of – and as a result of that, some things you might choose to do differently.

Let me explain.

Almost all organizations, no matter what sector or business they are in, operate in broadly the same way.

In a typical organization this is what happens. At the beginning of the year, the owners or shareholders or board decide that they want to do 'more' business as usual. They say they want to capture X percent more customers or market share, increase revenue by Y or profit by Z, sell such and such a percent more widgets and so on. They also want to do some brand new things – new products, services, initiatives, take different directions.

The management team takes this mission and launches a bunch of projects designed to make sure that both of these major thrusts (business as usual and new initiatives) are realized. Accompanying these two thrusts, they often say many of the things we mentioned already in the chapter on common sense, in the section called 'Things don't get done if people don't do them'. These are the phrases like:

- 'That's just the culture here'.
- 'I don't want to hear anybody using the word "can't"'.

- 'We like a can-do attitude here'.
- 'You're going to have to learn to do more with less'.
- 'You're being inflexible'.
- 'You're not being a team player'.
- 'Is this plan based on a five-day week?'
- 'You're lucky to have a job'.
- 'We don't have time to plan it, just go do it'.
- 'We have no choice – we have to do it'.
- 'That's not the kind of attitude we want around here'.
- 'We want can-do people here'.
- 'I don't think you're suited to the culture of this organization'.

While some of these phrases may sound quite different from each other, they in fact all have common undertones. These undertones are:

- What we're being asked to do is really tough.
- But it's certainly doable.
- And we know you're the man/woman for the job.
- And if you say you can't do it, you're being disloyal in some way.
- And planning is for wimps – the way to get this done is just to go in and do it.

Everybody in the organization now has (a) maybe a day job and (b) almost certainly, a project-related workload. People are 'multitasking' – that beloved phrase of most managers – working on several (or maybe many, many) things at once.

Most management teams expect everybody to undertake this workload. For this reason planning becomes somewhat secondary. Indeed planning can come to be viewed as something of a problem. After all, we don't want plans showing us that the things we are trying to do are impossible, now do we?

Because plans are non-existent or inadequate, there is no real measure of whether there are enough people to do all the work. (You may have heard the old saw, 'if you can't measure it, you can't manage it'). The suspicion (or it could be much stronger than that) is that there aren't. But it doesn't matter – because somehow, the view is, we'll find a way.

In reality, that 'somehow' is generally pretty obvious and well known to everybody. If there aren't enough people to do all the work, then the existing people can just work harder. And this is exactly what happens – the troops begin to work harder and harder, longer and longer hours.

Despite this, something – either a project or some business as usual thing – starts to drift. (This is inevitable if there aren't enough people to do all the work.) Eventually – it's usually as late as possible because nobody wants to be seen to be the bearer of bad news – somebody realizes that there's a problem.

When this happens there's a bit of a stink. Some senior manager or customer begins to jump up and down about their thing. If they shout loud enough people are switched onto that thing and the thing that lost the people is told to work even harder.

They do work harder – but it doesn't make any difference. That or some other thing now starts to drift, despite the long hours being worked. And the thing to which people were moved doesn't necessarily speed up. (If you're in any doubt about that Google

'Brooks' Law'.) There are learning curves and people need to come up to speed and they make mistakes that people who were already familiar with the thing had stopped making ages ago.

Life carries on like this until management realizes that something else is drifting. The same events occur – a stink, jumping up and down, people being moved from one thing to another, the progress on more and more things not being what was expected. And so the year unfolds with multitasking, nasty surprises – the phenomenon known as 'constantly changing priorities' and so-called 'fire fighting' becoming pretty much standard operating procedure.

Eventually the end of the year comes round. Some things have been done, many haven't. Many have come in late and/or over budget. Lots have been achieved only with superhuman effort. There is a sense that there has been a lot of wasted time, effort, resources or money. Right up to the last minute it's perhaps not been a 100% clear which things – out of all the things we set out to do at the beginning of the year – were going to end up being done and which were going to be left undone.

And were the things that got done the things that mattered most? Maybe. But maybe not. In the end there was no conscious decision making about this. It wasn't really the management that decided. It was decided more by the series of events that unfolded.

In other words – Fate/luck/chance.

Some people are burnt out and leave. Everybody thinks it's been a tough year and that they worked really hard. There is a sense of having triumphed in the face of adversity. We sure earned our salaries and bonuses this year, we think. Yep – we did one hell of a job. And there is a feeling that while the way we do things at that moment may not be perfect, it's the best way there is. These things just described are believed to be 'part of the culture of the organization'.

Now, if any of this sounded familiar, and if you don't want to become part of the madness, then the way to do that is through good planning. Do what it says in the chapter, *Projects and Getting Stuff Done*, and you'll be safe.

Don't – and you'll just join all the other lemmings – running around frantically and not having a life.

And if by some unfortunate quirk of fate, you happen to be the boss of such a place, a boss who thought you were running your organization and now you're not so sure, then here's the place to start. You need to look at how much work you're trying to do and how much people you have to do that work. Measure both in person-days and prepare to be surprised. (There's more about how to do this in my book, *Why A Little Planning Beats A Lot of Firefighting*.[37]

In summary, it's been my experience that there's something missing from many companies. I find it missing most often in knowledge-based and high-tech companies.

To use a fancy term, it's called capacity planning – more simply, knowing how much stuff you're trying to do and whether you have enough people to do all that stuff. It's the kind of thing that supposedly low-tech businesses – any shop in your high street, your local car mechanic, any manufacturing business – not only take for granted, but would laugh uproariously at the notion that you might *not* do it.

Watch out for it. It can be a killer. Don't become a victim of it.

PRESENTATIONS

YOU DON'T NEED TO BE LED BY POWERPOINT

A wise man speaks because he has something to say, a fool speaks because he has to say something.

– Plato, Greek philosopher

In 1980, in my first real management job, I had to do a presentation to the senior management of the place where I worked for a significant piece of capital expenditure. To do this I put my presentation together on paper and then went to a specialist company that converted it into 35-mm slides. It took the guts of a week to get it all done.

Today, with PowerPoint, the same job could be done in a few hours. So our lives are immeasurably better as a result, right?

Well . . . er, no . . . actually.

The phrase 'death by PowerPoint' has become a cliché. We've all sat through them – mind-numbingly boring slides, full of bulleted points and box diagrams and ludicrous levels of animation. If you haven't seen it before, check out this http://norvig.com/Gettysburg/ – the Gettysburg address in PowerPoint.

If I see a PowerPoint presentation, I read each slide, I don't listen to the guy (or gal) and then I'm going, 'Okay, next slide'. The presenter may as well not be there. Put on the slide show, sit down and let it run.

As discussed already in the chapter on meetings, it's often the culture of the organization that leads us to believe that we have to put together a massive slide deck. This is the way it's always been done so this is what's expected.

But it's ok to challenge this.

When you're putting together your presentation, use some common sense. See it from the audience's point of view. How would you feel if you were on the receiving end of your own presentation? Would it cause you to engage with the speaker? Would it give you useful information in a stimulating way? Or is it going to bore the pants off you? If the latter, you need to think again.

> 'So we must work at our profession and not make anybody else's idleness an excuse for our own. There is no lack of readers and listeners; it is for us to produce something worth being written and heard'.
>
> **– Pliny the Younger, Roman lawyer and author**

If you are going to do a presentation, here's what you need to remember:

1. If you are going to use up a few hours of people's precious time then *you'd better have a damn good reason for doing so.* In return for their time, you'd better be planning to give them something pretty bloody useful.
2. Ditch the PowerPoint. Or if that would feel too scary, if you couldn't conscience the thought of pressing the 'Off' button on the projector, then think of it as being like the handout. It contains the material you're going to cover but it's not going to be the centrepiece of what you do.
3. Give them the takeaway in the first 30 seconds. Essentially say to them – 'If you stay for the rest of my presentation, here will be the benefit to you'. You want it that if someone gets called away from the presentation, they will feel they have missed something significant.

4. Take them through the detail. Try and make it light if you can – even if it's a dull subject. See if you can make some jokes, tell war stories. If you don't know any jokes or have any stories, hunt around on the internet and find some. Within reason, feel free to embellish/exaggerate a little to make your point.

5. The worst thing you can do is read from a script like politicians do. Referring to notes is an improvement on reading from a script but the best thing of all is to do it as though it were off the cuff – as if you were making it up as you went along. This can be done. It takes lots of practice but whenever I speak I always try to do it. I teach an entire two-day course this way. It's just taken a lot of practice. I find mind mapping a good way to help me remember but if you were an amateur (or professional) actor, I imagine that would help tremendously.

6. If you're naturally shy, don't worry. Just imagine you're speaking to one person in the audience. So pick different people in turn and make like you're talking to them.

7. And for heaven's sake, don't talk to the screen that your slides (if you're using them) are appearing on, that is, with your back to, or turned sideways to the audience. Equally, if you're using a flipchart, don't turn your back to write. Stand at the side of the flipchart, sideways to the audience (but still looking at them) and write. This can be done too. Once again, it just takes a little practice.

8. Finally, remind the audience of the take away and what they can do with that – the benefit to them – why it was a good investment of their time to have come to your presentation.

9. That's all.

So in summary: find a way to engage with the audience (no matter how dull the subject is), reconsider your use of PowerPoint – and then send them away feeling that the time they spent listening to you was time damn well spent.

> '*A good speech should be like a woman's skirt; long enough to cover the subject and short enough to create interest*'.
>
> – Winston Churchill, former British Prime Minister

PROJECTS AND GETTING STUFF DONE

WHY YOU'RE PROBABLY BEING MISTAKEN FOR SANTA CLAUS

The secret of getting ahead is getting started. The secret of getting started is breaking your complex overwhelming tasks into small manageable tasks, and then starting on the first one.

– Mark Twain, American author

The boss calls you into her office, gathers up a pile of papers, hands them to you and says, 'Congratulations, this is your next project. Sales have promised it'll be delivered to the customer by September 30, the scope is set in the contract, it's a fixed price contract so that means the budget is fixed and – by the way – you can't hire any more people'.

It's the start of a million projects.

What happens next? You say, 'Sure', take the stuff and go. You start sending emails, allocating or hiring people, holding meetings, brainstorming, making phone calls . . .

Whoa there pardner!

Imagine you took your car to the garage and you said to the guy in the garage, 'I don't know what's wrong with my car but I need you to fix it in the next hour and I'll pay you fifty pounds', and he said 'Sure'.

Imagine you weren't feeling very well, you went to the doctor and you said, 'Doc, I'm not feeling very well. Fix me now and I'll give your forty euros for the visit', and he said 'Sure'.

Imagine you said to a builder, 'I'd like you to build me a house and the budget's $200,000', and he said 'Sure'.

Nobody (in their right mind) says 'Sure'. Yet in many industries (especially knowledge and high-tech industries), people routinely say it. It's mad!

If you're in the business of being handed projects to execute (and let's face it, who isn't?), then there's something you've got to understand. When they give you the project and say things like, 'This is the delivery date' or 'The budget's already been fixed' or 'You've got to do it with your existing team' or similar, you have to understand that this is nothing more than a letter to Santa Claus.

A what?

A letter to Santa Claus. Let me explain.

We've all – when we were kids (or maybe even more recently) – written letters to Santa where we've said, 'Dear Santa, this is the stuff I'd really like for Christmas . . .'. And then I'm sure we've all had the experience – even if we had very rich parents – of coming down on Christmas morning to find that we got some of the stuff we asked for but we probably didn't get all of it.

Because the world isn't like that – where we can just say, 'Here's what I want' and we get it.

> 'Bad planning on your part does not constitute an emergency on my part'.
> – Proverb

The world of business is no different. There may be perfectly valid business reasons why they're asking for these things. (There generally are. It's in the contract. Sales have sold it. The boss has promised it. Marketing has announced it. We need to book the revenue in the quarter. And so on and so on and so on. Generally, our bosses aren't just out to make our lives a misery with these requests.) But if a thing can't be done, you need to say so. And then – as we've mentioned previously – you need to say what *can* be done. Perhaps you can't give them an Xbox for Christmas but you can give them something else.

The way we to do that is, quite simply, to build a plan. Then, using the plan, you can see what's achievable and what's not achievable – which you can then use to renegotiate the initial request as needed, instead of just saying 'yes' to the task straight away.

What's in a plan?

A plan consists of five things:

1. What (precisely) are you trying to do?
2. What jobs have to be done to get to #1?
3. Who's going to make sure the jobs gets done?
4. Who's going to do those jobs in #2?
5. What are we going to do when things don't turn out as expected?

A plan ends up being built around four parameters or factors:

- **WHAT** – What are we trying to do?
- **WHEN** – When will it be done?
- **WORK** – The amount of work involved in getting the thing done.
- **QUALITY** – There are jobs in the plan which are about ensuring the quality of what gets delivered. These are things like testing, reviews, quality assurance, signoffs and so on.

By varying the four parameters you can come up with different ways to satisfy the boss's letter to Santa Claus.

So let's say, for example, that the project has to be done by a certain date. This is what the boss has told you; this is her letter to Santa.

Then maybe you can't give them everything she needs by that date, but you can offer a partial solution. Or maybe you can hit the date but you need more people or a bigger budget in order to do that. And so on. You can offer these different choices.

Ideally, you can give them that Xbox for Christmas. But if you can't, the plan will keep you honest. It will stop you from promising something you can't deliver. After all, you don't want your boss to come down on Christmas morning and find that Santa didn't come at all and that they've got an empty stocking.

And so ...

When you get handed that next project, don't say 'Sure' and run off and start doing stuff. Take a little time out. Build a plan. It won't take you that long. In fact I think you'll be surprised at how much you can get done in a short space of time. Then go talk to your boss.

And finally, if you want any more information on how to build a plan, I can highly recommend my book, *What You Need To Know About Project Management*.[38]

I'm probably better known for my destructive tendencies on the Discovery Channel's MythBusters *than anything else. You've seen us blow up cement trucks, create an earthquake machine and even seen us try to get old Chevys to fly, but behind all of that havoc is a lot of discipline and drive – brainstorming, creativity, research, planning, budgeting, project management.*

– Jamie Hyneman, American special effects expert, Villanova University commencement speech, 5 May 2010[39]

REPORTS AND REPORTING

WHY THIS IS YOUR CHANCE TO SAVE SOME RAINFOREST

Many intelligence reports in war are contradictory; even more are false, and most are uncertain.

– Carl von Clausewitz, German general and military theorist

S ome reports that get written provide vital information to the organization, enabling it to spot trends, identify opportunities, scan for threats, monitor project progress and so on. Some reports have to be written because of legal or regulatory requirements. And some reports get written . . . well, just because they get written.

You know that report that you spend all that time on? You have to gather data from different places. You have to go to meetings to get information. You have to cross-reference different files or databases.

It may be that at the end of all that, nobody reads it.

Somebody on a course I taught recently told me the following story. I have reproduced it here without an ounce of exaggeration. There was a report they used to write and which got sent out to *50* people. They stopped sending it just to see what would happen. *One* person came to them asking where it was. And that one person was the person who was previously responsible for preparing the same report and so clearly felt some sort of emotional attachment to it.

Again, don't misquote or misunderstand me. I'm not saying reports aren't important. But, in my experience, a lot of reports don't get read.

Project status reports are a great example of this. Each team member spends several hours every week writing a status report explaining what they did on the project. Tasks completed this week. Tasks planned for next week. Percentage complete. Critical issues. You know the kind of thing. Often this is information that the project manager could have found out just by walking around and talking to people. Or at a quick status meeting. If I'm a project manager and I have a choice between my team members working on getting the project done or writing status reports, I know which one I would want them to do.

So the message of this chapter is short and simple. People may read your report and it may provide invaluable information.

Or they may not and it may not. In which case, it's a waste of your time to be writing it.

If you have any suspicion at all that your report falls into the latter category, there's only one way to find out. It's pretty much the same as with meetings. Don't do it and see what happens.

If the sky falls you have your answer and if the sky doesn't fall . . . well, you know.

There are a few standard tests for whether people are reading your report or not. The most entertaining is to insert a sentence which reads, 'If you read this sentence I'll give you twenty euros/ pounds/ dollars' and then see if anybody comes looking for the money. This isn't my idea. This is an old idea but the number of people I've said this to and who have replied, 'Yeah, I've done that and nobody ever looked for any money from me'.

The second test is to send out last week's report with the date changed and see what happens. I've had somebody tell me that they were doing that for *12* weeks with a weekly report before anybody noticed. At best, such a report should be stopped altogether; at worst, it should only be going out once a quarter.

And finally, the third (and laziest) test. Just stop sending it and see if anybody notices.

Related to all of this is another possibility – that even if the report is necessary, it may not be necessary in its current unwieldy form. (An unwieldy form which has often been around since the Flood and just passed on from one generation to the next.) That giant 50-page tome that you spend so much time assembling every week could perhaps be replaced by something shorter, simpler, snappier and more streamlined – ideally a one-pager.

You might even get some brownie points by doing the streamlining. Just because things have been done a certain way in the past doesn't mean they always have to be done that way.

IBM used to (and maybe still do, for all I know) have a motto that said 'Think'. It's actually not bad advice.

> *'I don't think the intelligence reports are all that hot. Some days I get more out of the* New York Times*'.*
> – John F. Kennedy, 35th President of the United States

STARTING YOUR OWN THING

JUST GET OUT THERE AND SEE IF PEOPLE WILL BUY IT

Business opportunities are like buses, there's always another one coming.

– Sir Richard Branson, British entrepreneur

I f you decide to start your own business, one of the things you may do is get a bank loan or go after one of the many grant packages that are available. In either case you'll need a business plan. You'll need to explain your market research which leads you to believe you have a viable business. You'll then need to do projections based on that research. Doing the projections, you'll find yourself walking the high wire between:

- trying to be realistic/conservative but in reality appearing downbeat about your prospects, thereby underselling the business and not getting your loan/grant; and
- being upbeat but then running the risk of having what bankers like to call 'telephone numbers' in your proposal – and being turned down for that reason.

It's a tricky and, quite frankly, a tedious business. But it's the way the game is played. If you want to be in the club (of start-up entrepreneurs) then you have to play the game.

Now, with (almost no) due respect to bankers, they're a species I've tried to steer clear of for most of my entrepreneurial life. And as for grants, I've found personally, that the time I spent chasing the grant would have been far better spent chasing business. (But please understand that I'm not shooting down grants. It's just that I haven't found them to be particularly useful myself. And as for bankers . . .)

But what I discovered is that there's another way to start a business and I stumbled on it quite by accident. Here's what happened to me.

My original start your own business idea was simple. There were plenty of people out in the world selling project management as rocket science. I believed there was a market for project management as common sense. So in 1992, I set up my company – ETP – a project management training and consulting company. I put together a five-day project management course based around my common sense method for project management and start to hawk my wares.

A friend of mine, who was running a software company in the United States, gave me my first job. I flew to the States over the weekend and on Monday I taught the first day of the five-day course. It went down well. As we ended that day and were all saying our 'see you tomorrows', everyone seemed dead happy. Everyone except me that was.

The trouble was that I had taught *all* my material. Yep, *all* of it. The slides and stuff that I had thought would see me through five days had lasted one. I was through them all. Every single one.

What the hell was I to do?

That night I could only think of one thing. Since I had no more material, my only other option was to see if any of the people in the class had any. And of course, I realized they did – they had their projects. So I decided that that's what we would spend Tuesday doing – applying what they had learned from my course to *their* projects. That would take care of Tuesday. If I could get through Tuesday, then I would worry about Wednesday, Thursday and Friday.

But happily, the issues we uncovered on Tuesday – applying the method to their projects – kept us going right to the end of the week. We were even a bit stuck for time at the end. The course was a big success, there was some money in the bank, a satisfied international customer and some great endorsements. We were up and running.

Back at base, I learned the lessons. I rapidly slimmed the five-day course down to three days. And the idea of applying my method to their projects became a central idea that is still there today. Indeed, it has become the backbone of all the training we do. People love it. It solves real problems. They do 'real work' on the course as well as learning a vital skill – project management.

What did I learn?

I learnt two vital lessons.

The first one was that once you set up your business, there's only one piece of market research that – IMHO – is of any value. You can do all the surveys, focus groups, analysis of data and trends, quantification of the size of the market that you like, but – in the end – only one thing matters. Is there somebody prepared to pay money for your product? If there is then you're in business.

And the second thing I learned is that what you've put out there initially may not be quite right. In fact it may a long way off being quite right. But once it's out there, you can start to iterate it and make it better – bringing it closer to the thing that solves the customer's problem.

So these days, when I have a new idea for a product or service – essentially starting a new mini-business – I do the following:

- Put together what I think the product or service should be.
- Try and sell it.

I have a folder on my computer called 'Stuff That Never Worked'. It's a *big* folder. It contains a whole bunch of things that I tried and that failed. I came up with what I thought was a great idea, made something I could sell, tried to sell it and nobody bought.

That's okay, though. I had put minimal effort, time and money into it. I could move on swiftly to the next great thing.

> *You cannot tell from appearances how things will go. Sometimes imagination makes things out far worse than they are; yet without imagination not much can be done. Those people who are imaginative see many more dangers than perhaps exist; certainly many more than will happen; but then they must also pray to be given that extra courage to carry this far-reaching imagination.*
>
> – Winston Churchill, former British Prime Minister, speech at Harrow School in 1941[40]

And you know what the nicest thing of all is? It turns out that this idea of make something and iterate it, that I accidentally stumbled on and figured out for myself, has actually become respectable. So respectable that even the *Harvard Business Review*[41] expounds on it – and you don't get much more respectable than that.

The process is known as 'lean start-up' and was developed initially by Eric Ries. Google the term 'lean start-up' and you can find out all about it. You could also buy – and if you're thinking of starting a business, you absolutely should buy – Eric Ries's best-selling book,

The Lean Start-up: How Today's Entrepreneurs Use Continuous Innovation to Create Radically Successful Businesses.[42]

Here you'll learn about things like:

- Minimal viable product. (Do I need to spell it out?)
- Continuous deployment – what I called 'finding customers'.
- Split testing – offering customers two different versions of the same product to see which sells better.
- Actionable metrics – sensible measures that can guide you to where you should go next with your product development.

So if you've got a great idea and you're thinking of starting a business, yeah sure, you could go do the round of business plans, banks and grants.

Or you could just make something and see if people will buy it.

I know which I think makes more sense.

How will you use your gifts?
What choices will you make?

Will inertia be your guide, or will you follow your passions?

Will you follow dogma, or will you be original?

Will you choose a life of ease, or a life of service and adventure?

Will you wilt under criticism, or will you follow your convictions?

Will you bluff it out when you're wrong, or will you apologize?

Will you guard your heart against rejection, or will you act when you fall in love?

Will you play it safe, or will you be a little bit swashbuckling?

When it's tough, will you give up, or will you be relentless?

Will you be a cynic, or will you be a builder?

Will you be clever at the expense of others, or will you be kind?

I will hazard a prediction. When you are 80 years old, and in a quiet moment of reflection narrating for only yourself the most personal version of your life story, the telling that will be most compact and meaningful will be the series of choices you have made. In the end, we are our choices. Build yourself a great story.

– Jeff Bezos, founder of Amazon, Princeton University commencement speech, 30 May 2010[43]

Epilogue

As you can imagine, I watched a lot of commencement speeches in the course of writing this book. Some were humdrum, some were funny – often hilariously so – some really *were* inspirational. Some surprised me – people I thought would have a lot to say and say it well – and who, IMHO, did neither of these things.

There are two I would want to take with me to a desert island, two that I would happily sit through any time.

One was my all-time favourite – the late Steve Jobs at Stanford.[21]

The other – and a close second – was a wonderful one by Admiral William H. McRaven of the US Navy. McRaven commanded the US Special Forces mission against Osama bin Laden. You might not like the somewhat peremptory tone of it – he can be forgiven, I guess, he's been in the military for thirty odd years – but there's no disagreeing with the sentiments. Here's how he concludes, summing up his speech – and indeed, much of what has been said in this book.

*But, YOU are the
class of 2014 – the class that can affect the
lives of 800 million people in the next century.*

Start each day with a task completed.

Find someone to help you through life.

Respect everyone.

*Know that life is not fair and that you will fail often,
but if you take some risks, step up when the times are
toughest, face down the bullies, lift up the downtrodden
and never, ever give up – if you do these things, then the
next generation and the generations that follow will live in
a world far better than the one we have today and – what
started here will indeed have changed the world – for the
better.*

William H. McRaven, US Navy Admiral, University of
Texas at Austin commencement speech,
May 2014[44]

References

1 Lloyd Blankfein commencement speech, http://www.business insider.com/lloyd-blankfeins-graduation-speech-2013–6.

2 *Ithaca* by C.P. Cavafy, https://www.youtube.com/watch?v=1n3n2Ox4Yfk.

3 Jon Bon Jovi commencement speech, http://bluehawk.monmouth.edu/~opa/commencement/jbjSpeech.html.

4 Barbara Desoer commencement speech, http://haas.berkeley.edu/news/2011commencementdesoer.html.

5 O'Connell, Fergus, *The Power of Doing Less*, Capstone, 2013.

6 Ferriss, Timothy, *The 4-Hour Work Week: Escape the 9–5, Live Anywhere and Join the New Rich*, Vermillion, 2011.

7 Jill Geisler commencement speech, http://www.poynter.org/how-tos/leadership-management/what-great-bosses-know/184425/the-10-powers-of-leadership-and-why-they-matter/.

8 Murray, W.H., *The Scottish Himalayan Expedition*, Dent, 1951.

9 O'Connell, Fergus, *Simply Brilliant: The Common-Sense Guide to Success at Work,* Pearson, 2012.

10 John F. Kennedy civil rights speech, http://www.americanrhetoric.com/speeches/jfkcivilrights.htm.

11 Huntford, Roland, *Scott and Amundsen: The Last Place on Earth*, Abacus, 2000.

12 Adams, Scott, *Telling It Like It Isn't*, Boxtree, 1997.

13 Maria Shriver commencement speech, https://www.youtube
.com/watch?v=A5xLcLIlXqU.

14 http://www.theguardian.com/music/musicblog/2013/apr/26/
james-rhodes-blog-find-what-you-love.

15 Oprah Winfrey commencement speech, http://news.stanford
.edu/news/2008/june18/como-061808.html.

16 Jeffers, Susan, *Feel The Fear And Do It Anyway*, Vermilion,
2007.

17 Jim Carrey commencement speech, https://www.youtube
.com/watch?v=4AOQgrNKLWM#t=13.

18 'Failure Wall' Inspires Success, http://www.cnbc.com/
id/46101756.

19 J.K. Rowling commencement speech, https://www.youtube
.com/watch?v=wHGqp8lz36c.

20 Conan O'Brien commencement speech, https://www.youtube
.com/watch?v=5cFY0-IFcwc (Part 1) and https://www.youtube
.com/watch?v=ErZVczhKIss (Part 2).

21 Steve Jobs commencement speech, http://www.youtube.com/
watch?v=VHWUCX6osgM.

22 http://www.marieforleo.com/2014/04/find-your-passion/.

23 https://www.youtube.com/watch?v=pjkLf_X88WM.

24 Kaufman, Josh, *The First 20 Hours: How to Learn Anything
Fast*, Portfolio Penguin, 2013.

25 http://www.inc.com/ss/america039s-weirdest-businesses#1.

26 http://www.marieforleo.com/2013/10/bridge-job/.

27 Sir Richard Branson commencement speech, http://britrish
.com/2013/05/21/richard-bransons-commencement-speech/.

28 Simon Sinek on why people buy, https://www.youtube.com/
watch?v=qp0HIF3SfI4.

29 Mandino, Og, *The Greatest Salesman in the World*, Jaico,
2008.

30 Sheryl Sandberg commencement speech, http://barnard.edu/headlines/transcript-and-video-speech-sheryl-sandberg-chief-operating-officer-facebook.

31 Bradley Whitford commencement speech, http://www.news.wisc.edu/9829.

32 Covey, Stephen, *The 7 Habits of Highly Effective People*, Simon & Schuster, 2004.

33 Carnegie, Dale, *How to Win Friends and Influence People,* Vermilion, 2006.

34 Bill Nye commencement speech, http://bostinno.streetwise.co/2014/05/17/transcript-of-bill-nye-2014-commencement-speech-at-umass-lowell/.

35 Robert Krulwich commencement speech, http://blogs.discovermagazine.com/notrocketscience/2011/05/12/there-are-some-people-who-dont-wait-robert-krulwich-on-the-future-of-journalism/#.U5QRmpRdVZ0.

36 Carol Bartz commencement speech, http://www.businessinsider.com/carol-bartzs-uw-madison-graduation-speech-2012-5.

37 O'Connell, Fergus, *Why A Little Planning Beats A Lot of Fire-fighting*, Little Brown, Spring 2015.

38 O'Connell, Fergus, *What You Need To Know About Project Management*, Capstone, 2011.

39 Jamie Hyneman commencement speech, http://www.discovery.com/tv-shows/mythbusters/about-this-show/jamie-hyneman-commencement.htm.

40 Winston Churchill speech at Harrow, http://www.school-for-champions.com/speeches/churchill_never_give_in.htm#.U5QZYZRdVZ0.

41 http://hbr.org/2013/05/why-the-lean-start-up-changes-everything/ar/1.

42 Ries, Eric, *The Lean Start-up: How Today's Entrepreneurs Use Continuous Innovation to Create Radically Successful Businesses*, Portfolio Penguin, 2011.

43 Jeff Bezos commencement speech, http://www.business insider.com/we-are-what-we-choose-2010-6.

44 Admiral William McRaven commencement speech http://jimdaly.focusonthefamily.com/navy-seals-commencement-speech-full-of-common-sense-wisdom/.

Acknowledgements

A huge thank you, as always, to my redoubtable and tireless agent, Darin Jewell. As the years go by and we do more and more projects together, I bless the day when he called me up and said, 'I'd like to represent you'.

Thank you to my colleagues, Karen Fahy and Val Downey. I haven't thanked them for a few books now but it's worth saying again. They keep the ETP engine purring.

I'm grateful to all of the team at Wiley – Vicky Kinsman, Jonathan Shipley, Emma Henshall, Megan Saker, Laura Cooksley, Samantha Hartley – for their support, help, creativity, suggestions, pushing me to up my game and ferociously hard work.

Most of all though, at Wiley I want to single out the wonderful Jenny Ng. This is the third book she and I have done together and I can't think of anyone I'd rather have as my co-pilot when we set off on one of these adventures.

Finally I'd like to thank Terri Campbell and Richard Gough for their generous help.

About the Author

The *Sunday Business Post* has described Fergus O'Connell (www .fergusoconnell.com) as having 'more strings to his bow than a Stradivarius'.

His 2002 novel, *Call the Swallow,* was described by *The Irish Times* as 'better than *Schindler's Ark*' (itself a Booker Prize winner). *Call the Swallow* was short listed for the 2002 Kerry Ingredients Irish Fiction Prize and nominated for the Hughes & Hughes/Sunday Independent Novel of the Year.

Since 2009 he has been writing his *The Four Lights* quartet of love stories. All four novels in the series – *Starlight, Sunlight, Moonlight* and *Candlelight* – have now been published. He is currently work- ing on a new novel.

Fergus has a First in Mathematical Physics from University College Cork and is one of the world's leading authorities on project man- agement. His company – ETP (www.etpint.com)—and his project management method – The Ten Steps – have influenced a gen- eration of project managers. In 2003 this method was used to plan and execute the Special Olympics World Games, the world's biggest sporting event that year. Fergus's experience covers inter- national projects; he has taught project management in Europe, North America, South America and Asia. He has written on the subject for many publications including the *Wall Street Journal*. He has lectured at University College Cork, Trinity College Dublin, Dublin Institute of Technology, Bentley College, Boston University, the Michael Smurfit Graduate School of Business and on television for the National Technological University. He holds two patents.

Fergus is the author of 13 business and self-help books (http://www.amazon.com/Fergus-OConnell/e/B000APF0KK/ref=ntt_athr_dp_pel_1). The first of these, *How to Run Successful Projects – The Silver Bullet*, has become both a bestseller and a classic and has been constantly in print for over 20 years. His book on common sense entitled *Simply Brilliant* – also a bestseller and now in its fourth edition – was runner-up in the W.H. Smith Book Awards 2002. His books have been translated into 23 languages.

Fergus has also written a book on project management for children. Entitled, *How To Put A Man On The Moon If You're A Kid*, it is one of a pair of books to teach the essential skills of project management and time management to schoolchildren. (The other – *How To Build Rome In A Day If You're A Kid* – will be published in 2015.)

He has two children and now lives in Ireland.

About ETP, Fergus's company

ETP (www.etpint.com) is a company, founded by Fergus O'Connell, which specializes in programme and project management for knowledge and high-tech industries.

If – like us – you believe that:

- Project management is not rocket science but rather, common sense.
- 'Light' project management is the best project management.
- A little planning beats a lot of firefighting.
- Projects should get done as cheaply as possible with minimum waste.
- No project should ever fail.
- We should always be working on the most important things.
- An organization should maximize its capacity to deliver projects
- We should make every project day count
- Project personnel can and should have a life outside work,

then we should be working together.

For consultancy, training or speaking at your event, you can contact Fergus at fergus.oconnell@etpint.com.

Also by
Fergus O'Connell

Fiction

Call The Swallow

The Four Lights Quartet:

1 Starlight
2 Sunlight
3 Moonlight
4 Candlelight

Non-fiction

How To Run Successful Projects – The Silver Bullet, 3rd edition

How To Run Successful High-Tech Project-Based Organizations

How To Run Successful Projects In Web-Time

Simply Brilliant – The Competitive Advantage of Common Sense, 3rd edition

How To Do A Great Job – And Go Home On Time

Fast Projects: Project Management When Time Is Short

How To Get More Done: Seven Days to Achieving More

ALSO BY FERGUS O'CONNELL

Work Less, Achieve More: Great Ideas to Get Your Life Back

Earn More, Stress Less: How To Attract Wealth Using the Secret Science of Getting Rich

What You Need To Know About Project Management

Zero Waste In Business

The Power of Doing Less: Why Time Management Courses Don't Work and How to Spend Your Precious Life on the Things That Really Matter

Books for children

How To Put A Man On The Moon If You're A Kid

You Can Contact Me

You can email me at Fergus.oconnell@etpint.com.

I have a website www.fergusoconnell.com.

I have a Facebook page http://www.facebook.com/fergusoconell where I talk about lots of different stuff including my latest writing projects. I'm on Twitter @TheTaff.

And if you liked the book, maybe you'd be kind enough to write a review on the Amazon product page.

get more

Your monthly dose of business brilliance - articles, interviews, videos and more

Sign up to our newsletter today!